Surviving Adolescence

Jim Burns

Regal

A Division of Gospel Light
Ventura, California, U.S.A.

Published by Regal Books
A Division of Gospel Light
Ventura, California, U.S.A.
Printed in U.S.A.

Cover Design by Barbara LeVan Fisher
Interior Design by Britt Rocchio
Edited by David Webb and Virginia Woodard

Library of Congress Cataloging-in-Publication Data
Burns, Jim, 1953-
    Surviving adolescence / Jim Burns.
        p. cm.
    Summary: Discusses a variety of common problems that teenagers face and gives advice on how to cope with them from a Christian point of view.
    ISBN 0-8307-2065-0 (trade paper)
    1. Teenagers—Religious life—Juvenile literature. 2. Self-esteem in adolescence—Religious aspects—Christianity—Juvenile literature. 3. Teenagers—Conduct of life—Juvenile literature. 4. Christian life—Juvenile literature. 5. Adolescence—Juvenile literature. [1. Adolescence. 2. Self-esteem. 3. Christian life. 4. Conduct of life.]
I. Title.
    BV4531.2.B874 1997   97-22738
    248.8'3—dc21   CIP

1 2 3 4 5 6 7 8 9 10 11 12 13 14 15 16 17 18 19 20 / 04 03 02 01 00 99 98 97

Rights for publishing this book in other languages are contracted by Gospel Literature International (GLINT). GLINT also provides technical help for the adaptation, translation and publishing of Bible study resources and books in scores of languages worldwide. For further information, contact GLINT, P.O. Box 4060, Ontario, CA 91761-1003, U.S.A., or the publisher.

To my daughter
Rebecca Joy Burns

Daily you remind me of God's richest blessings.

Your wonderful smile, bear hugs and delightful,

sensitive spirit have brought me a deeper joy than you

will ever imagine. You are a miracle, a special gift

from God and a masterpiece in the making.

Love,
Dad

Contents

Acknowledgments

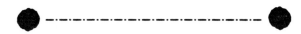

This book was a pure joy to write. It is filled with stories and principles that remind me once again of how fortunate Cathy and I are to have such a special network of friends. We are a family most blessed by many wonderful people. At the risk of overlooking key individuals involved in this project, I do want to acknowledge a few people without whose help and encouragement this book would still be but a dream.

Thank you, Cathy, for your amazingly positive attitude about this project, your encouragement that kept me going and your consistent Christian lifestyle. Christy, Rebecca and Heidi saw less of their Daddy during this time, yet brought the needed doses of joy and reality to remind me this was an important project. Special thanks go to our precious friends, Dale and Karen Walters, for their sacrificial and supportive friendship. Karen, thank you for putting up with my handwriting and for going the second, third and fourth mile to complete this project.

A very important part of any project of the National Institute of Youth Ministry and my life is the partnership I have with Jill Corey. Jill, thank you for your leadership at NIYM and for your desire to do quality ministry. Your handprint is all over our ministry.

Many thanks to Bob and Cleva Howard for your phenomenal support and encouragement. Thank you to Bill Greig III and Kyle Duncan at Regal Books and to all the wonderful people at Gospel Light for your friendship and partnership in our ministry.

> But those who hope in the Lord will renew their strength.
> They will soar on wings like eagles; they will run and not
> grow weary, they will walk and not be faint (Isaiah 40:31).

Jim Burns
Dana Point, California

To Parents and Youth Workers

We were *never* their age! True, we were 11, 12 and 13, but we were never *their* age. Today's teenager experiences so much at such a young age. The journey from childhood to adulthood—we call it adolescence—is sometimes frightening. It's moving from dependence on you to independence. Adolescence is a time of experimentation and exploration. It's dealing with life-forming and life-changing issues such as self-esteem, sex, dating, peer pressure, emotions, drugs and God. Your teenager and preteenager need you now more than ever to help them through the maze of adolescence.

Obviously, teens do grow up. They do "survive" adolescence in a physical sense. But some people never completely recover from the habits developed and emotions damaged during these formative years. Building a healthy, positive foundation during adolescence is no easy task. Yet it's vital for a meaningful adult life. During this critical period we must help kids to:

- Develop a sense of identity,
- Establish healthy relationships and
- Make life decisions.

That's what this book is all about. *Surviving Adolescence* is a book about choices. I'm attempting to help kids make positive decisions and prevent them from making negative ones. At the beginning of the book, I challenge young people to recognize that the decisions they make today will affect them for the rest of their lives.

This book was written as much for you as for your teenager(s). It's a book to help you and your teenager(s) reach adulthood safely. As you well know, there are no easy formulas or quick fixes when it comes to raising teenagers. Just when you think you are beginning to figure it out, the rules change! It takes hard work, an understanding of the teenage culture, perseverance and a desire to communicate in a sometimes alien environment. Is it worth the effort? Of course it is. There may be nothing more difficult, but nothing can be more rewarding than taking an active role in a young person's journey of discovery.

My hope is that you will read this book with your teenager and, together, begin to figure out the truly important issues in life. I have tried to make the book practical, full of stories, blunt (!) and based on Christian principles. In the study guide at the end of the book, I provide discussion starters for each chapter and suggest individual and group activities that will make for positive learning experiences. Kids learn best when they are interacting and discussing key points. Youth leaders may also find this book useful as curriculum.

Surviving Adolescence is probably the most important book I have yet written because it goes to the core of teen issues and challenges kids not to settle for second best. I'm convinced that if you will invest the time and energy to read this book with your teenager, you will do more than "survive adolescence." Together you will create an absolute masterpiece of a life. *Go for it!*

Jim Burns

Part One

Building a Healthy Self-Image

Learning to Like
Yourself

When I walked into Mrs. Chun's fourth-grade classroom on the first day of school, there was something unique about me. It wasn't something I was very proud of. In fact, this "uniqueness" caused me a great deal of trauma and embarrassment. You see, I was the only boy in the entire fourth grade at Horace Mann Elementary School in Anaheim, California, who had hair growing out of his armpits. (Actually, Priscilla Shelton also had hair under her arms, but that's another story!)

Now, this growth under my arms was not exactly a bush, mind you, but it was *hair*, and that was bad enough. In fourth grade, I wasn't sure I could ever show those hairs to anyone. The first time I remember praying was during that year when I begged God, "Please never let me be 'skins' when our basketball team plays 'shirts and skins.'" Whenever I raised my hand in class, I covered my armpit with my other hand.

You may be wondering what this story about a 10-year-old, hairy-armed boy has to do with surviving adolescence. Simply this: What has happened to you during your childhood years can have a large influence on how successfully you handle the years between the ages of 13 and 18. It has to do with how you feel about who you are, whether or not you like yourself.

The "armpit" story is just one traumatic experience from my past. If you had the time, I could tell you about many embarrassing incidents and other experiences that adversely affected the way I felt about myself during the adolescent years. We could talk about my childhood hurts, the times I succumbed to peer pressure and the feeling of not being accepted by so-called friends at school. Or we could just talk about the problems I had with my physical looks. If you think this wasn't a problem for me, turn the book over and look again at the back cover. My wife sure didn't marry me for my great hair, athletic physique or movie-star looks.

Some people call this low self-esteem. Ever since I can remember, I have played the comparison game—comparing myself to others

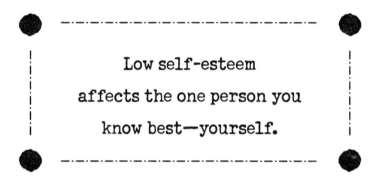

Low self-esteem
affects the one person you
know best—yourself.

around me. But whenever I play the comparison game, I always lose. Wherever I look I see people who are smarter, more coordinated, better looking and more talented than I. But the fact is that most of these same people (and most of the people you know) suffer from a poor self-image. It is likely that low self-esteem affects the one person you know best—yourself.

Your self-esteem, or self-image, is how you think and feel about yourself. And how you feel about yourself will affect *every part of your life*.

How you think and feel about yourself will determine much of your outlook on life, whether joyful, miserable, adventurous, tragic or indifferent. Your view of life will, in turn, color your relationships with friends, family and others. How these people respond to you takes you back to the beginning of the cycle—how they treat you will have a tremendous effect on how you think and feel about yourself. (See the diagram on page 15.')

Nicki always put herself down. Even when someone tried to compliment her on her hairstyle or clothes, she refused to accept the compliment at face value. She tended to be a complainer. Deep down inside she hated herself, knowing she was becoming a very negative person.

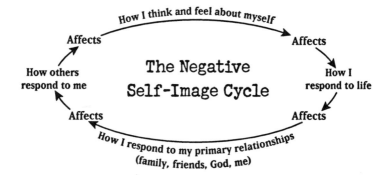

Nicki's parents nagged her not to be so critical of herself, but she couldn't get the negative thoughts out of her head. She didn't like her looks, and she hated her clothes. She felt that if she were taller she would be prettier. Nicki even hated her quiet personality. There were times she resented God for not making her a different person.

Nicki was caught in a vicious cycle of low self-esteem. She didn't like herself, and her negative outlook affected how others viewed and responded to her. Because most of her "vibes" were unfavorable toward others, she didn't receive a lot of positive support. Convinced that everyone hated her, she began to feel even worse about herself.

For Nicki to break the cycle she had to learn to like herself. Learning to like yourself is one of the keys to making your adolescent years a positive experience. That's what this book is all about.

You are an unrepeatable miracle. This may be hard to believe sometimes, but you are the making of a masterpiece. There is no one else quite like you in this entire world, and that makes you someone special.

Is it easy to overcome an inferiority complex? Can you learn to feel good about yourself in 10 simple lessons? The answer is an emphatic *NO*. When it comes to the struggles of life, no one said it was going to be easy. But I have great news for you. You *can* establish your own identity and learn to really like yourself. And the best news is that building a healthy self-image is not all left up to you.

The God who created this world cares deeply about who you are and who you are becoming. This is the way I figure it: To build a healthy self-image in you, God must do His part and you must do yours. God has already done His part, so all you have to do is respond to what He has already done for you.

God's Part:

- God created you;
- He loves you;
- He accepts you;
- He forgives you;
- He values you;
- He gifted you.

My daughter Rebecca Joy Burns was a real trip as a little girl. I was absolutely crazy about her...and still am! Once when she was almost four years old, I came home from a hard day at the office. All three of my girls were pretending to make pies—using real, live California mud! Christy and Heidi saw me, looked up and waved. Rebecca came running to me, and before I could get out of the way, she took a leap in the air and landed on my lap. I was wearing the only tie I own and my best suit of clothes. Rebecca was covered with mud, and now, so was I.

She said, "Daddy, you must be hungry and thirsty. I'll fix you something."

Afraid I'd be offered a mud pie, I quickly said, "Rebecca, I'm not hungry. I just want some water." After all, even a three-year-old can't mess up water.

Well, Rebecca climbed up to the cupboard to get a glass, leaving mud everywhere. (Incidentally, Cathy wasn't home or this never would have taken place). She took a clean, crystal glass to the sink, filled it with warm water and walked carefully toward me while water sloshed on the floor. She was so proud as she handed me the glass. When she handed it to me I noticed that two of her muddiest fingers were still in the glass of water, leaving little brown streaks running down the inside.

I took the warm (gross!) water with mud (double gross!) in the glass and held it in my hand. I looked at Rebecca; she was so excited that she had served her Daddy. I glanced at the disaster in the kitchen. I stared at the warm, muddy water, and I did what any loving father would do. I drank the water in one gulp!

What does this story have to do with God's part in building my healthy self-esteem? If a human father thinks enough of his little girl to drink warm, muddy water, then our heavenly Father who created me is even more devoted to wanting the best for me.

Let's expand on that. Because God created you, He loves you and accepts you as His child. Through Jesus Christ He forgives you. He values your relationship with Him enough to have sacrificed His only Son for you, so that you can have an abundant life on earth and an eternal relationship with God.

He gifted you with potential and abilities that will benefit His kingdom and make you a healthy, happy person. I've heard it said this way: "God don't sponsor no flops." God's part in helping you learn to like yourself is at the very core of your self-image.

Now the part you are to play emerges. To put it very simply, your response to what God has already done for you will make the difference between a positive or negative self-image.

Your Part:

- Put God first in your life.
- Live up to your potential.

Put God First in Your Life

Jesus said it best. "Seek first his kingdom and his righteousness, and all these things will be given to you as well" (Matthew 6:33). Jesus promises us that when we put God first, then our lives will be in order. Does He promise a problem-free life? No way. He does, however, offer to take care of us day by day when we make Him top priority in our lives.

People with low self-esteem have, first and foremost, a spiritual problem. Your relationship with God ultimately affects every other area of your life. When I tried to put God first, it affected my relationships with parents, friends, family members and even teachers. Putting God first had a tremendous effect on my grades, work, health and, very importantly, my dating relationships.

When you allow God's profound love and belief in you to be placed at the center of your life, you are well on your way to living up to your potential.

Living Up to Your Potential

With the Incarnate Power of the Universe loving you and caring for you, you are free to be all God desires you to be. Let me introduce you to a friend of mine. His name is Trevor Ferrell. He is 23 years old, and he lives life to the fullest.

Trevor lives in Philadelphia. When he was 11 years old, he happened to see a television news program about the street people of his city. Unable to understand how people could live without a home just a few miles from his own suburban community, he coaxed his parents that very night to take him to the inner city where the homeless lived. As Trevor witnessed the horrible conditions of the homeless on that cold, winter evening, he took his very own blanket and pillow and gave them to a man huddled on a subway grate in the freezing weather.

At the age of 11, Trevor Ferrell began a ministry called "Trevor's Army." With the help of his family and community, and with ever-increasing national support, he began to provide food, clothing and shelter for those who had no place to go.

Trevor is living up to his potential. He's making a difference. He told me once, "I am only one, but I am one; I can't do everything, but I can do something."

While Trevor was still a teenager, his actions and attitudes touched the hearts of millions of people. His story has been told in every major newspaper and magazine, and he has been seen on every major television network. He is the recipient of the John Roger Integrity Award, an honor given to both Mother Teresa and Mahatma Gandhi. His efforts also earned him recognition from the White House while he was still in his early teens.

Trevor knows how to live up to his potential and is making a difference. When you put God first, you can learn to like yourself and live life to the fullest.

Go for It:
Making Good Decisions

Last year's high school graduation ceremony was both a happy and sad occasion for me. As I walked past the graduating seniors of Corona del Mar High School, I realized I knew about half the class. Many of them I had known since their freshman year.

It was a happy time as I saw students who over those few years of high school had changed their direction in life for the better. During their high school years they had made a decision to be all that God wanted them to be. They didn't settle for second best in life. They were really going to be somebody.

It was also a sad time. Others I had known for four to six years had at one time been going in the right direction. Now, they were settling for mediocrity. Somewhere along the line they had walked away from God and His will for their lives. Some had been seduced by peer pressure. Others were more than casual drug and alcohol abusers. It was depressing to see people with so much potential settle for less than the best. A phrase kept running through my mind. *The decisions you make today play an important part in who you become in the future.*

I remember my 10-year high school reunion. As we pulled into the Disneyland Hotel parking lot, the same guys who drank beer in the parking lot before football games were there passing out cans of beer from the back of a pickup truck. The biggest flirt in my class had been married and divorced three times and had five kids. The young man voted most likely to succeed was already a very successful person 10 years later. I was elected "most likely to recede"—I'm talking about hair!—and 10 years later I had fulfilled the prophecy.

My point is that when these adults were teenagers they made decisions—some wise, some not so wise. They never dreamed that those decisions would affect them forever. Many of the decisions you make and habits you develop as a teen will stay with you for life. Many people in your school will settle for second best in life. They will decide that mediocrity is okay and will never reach their God-given potential. I hope you're not one of those people. Let me tell you one of my favorite stories.

> Once upon a time, in a land far away, there lived a group of people called the Laconians. The Laconians lived in a rural setting, their village surrounded by a forest. They looked and acted a lot like you and I. They dressed like we dress and went to school and work as we do. They experienced similar family struggles and search for identity. But there was one major difference: Connected to the ankle of every Laconian was a brace, and attached to the brace was a strong metal chain. And connected to the chain was a heavy, metal ball.
>
> Wherever the Laconians went, they carried the ball and chain. Yet no one seemed to mind. After all, they were used to the ball and chain, and no one in Laconia was free from bondage to the ball and chain.
>
> One day a young Laconian named Tommy was exploring in the forest after school. As he was hiking, he slipped and fell—and the chain broke. Tommy had never heard of a chain breaking before in the land of Laconia. He was terrified. But he was also curious. As he stood and stared at the broken chain he sensed that something very significant had happened. He tried to take a step without the ball and chain and almost fell down. After all, he wasn't used to the freedom of walking unfettered.
>
> Tommy slipped the ball and chain back on his ankle. He told no one of his new discovery. The next day after school his curiosity drove him back to the forest to experiment with his newfound freedom. This time when

he unhooked the chain he walked. Yes, it was wobbly at first, but he quickly learned to compensate. In a few hours, he was running and jumping and even trying to climb the trees in the forest. Every day after school he went to the forest, free to experience life in a different way from anyone else in Laconia.

He decided to share his secret with his best friend. After school one day, he brought his friend to the forest and demonstrated his newfound freedom. But his friend was appalled, saying, "Don't be different! You're a Laconian. You'll always be a Laconian. Be happy with what you have."

This response only threw fuel on Tommy's fire. He knew he needed to show all the people of his little village that they, too, could be free.

One spring day, when the whole village was outside, Tommy took the ball and placed it under his arm, then ran and skipped through the town. He wanted to share his joy and freedom with the people of his village. But the Laconians were outraged. They mocked Tommy and scolded him—and insisted that he not be different. Even his family demanded that he conform to the normal lifestyle of the community and replace his chain.

But Tommy knew that, having experienced freedom, he could never again settle for second best in life. For Tommy, mediocrity was out of the question. He would choose to be different...and he *was* different from then on.

I wrote this little story for people who don't want to settle for second best in life. What is keeping you from breaking the chains of this world and striving to be all that God wants you to be? Jesus said, "You will know the truth, and the truth will set you free" (John 8:32). You don't have to live a life of boring mediocrity. God's desire for your life is to break the chain that holds you back and to give your life over to His purpose. You can choose to be different!

My hope is that you *will* choose to be different. I hope at your age you will make positive decisions that will play an important part in determining who you are and who you will become in the future. My hope is that you will break the chain that keeps you from reaching your God-given potential. Life is short. Go for it!

In the New Testament, we find this story about a man who had been sick for at least 38 years:

> Some time later, Jesus went up to Jerusalem for a feast of the Jews. Now there is in Jerusalem near the Sheep Gate a pool, which in Aramaic is called Bethesda and which is surrounded by five covered colonnades. Here a great number of disabled people used to lie—the blind, the lame, the paralyzed. One who was there had been an invalid for thirty-eight years. When Jesus saw him lying there and learned that he had been in this condition for a long time, He asked him, "Do you want to get well?"
>
> "Sir," the invalid replied, "I have no one to help me into the pool when the water is stirred. While I am trying to get in, someone else goes down ahead of me."
>
> Then Jesus said to him, "Get up! Pick up your mat and walk." At once the man was cured; he picked up his mat and walked (John 5:1-9).

Imagine this scene for a moment in your mind. Picture a beautiful pool with large marble columns and perhaps exquisite works of art all around it. Now envision sick people with every imaginable illness sitting and lying beside the pool. Some have been there for years and years. They have been waiting for the periodic stirring of the water in the pool. These people believed that an angel of the Lord would come and heal the first person to step into the pool when the water was stirred. It must have been quite a sight.

The star of our story had been an invalid for 38 long years. For some reason, Jesus picked out this man and went straight to him. Jesus asked the man a very important question, "Do you want to get well?"

It seemed that there should be an obvious answer to this straightforward question. However, the invalid didn't answer yes. He hesitated and then made an excuse. Jesus didn't respond to the man's excuse but continued, "Get up! Pick up your mat and walk."

At once the man was healed. He picked up his mat and walked for the first time in 38 years.

You and I are a lot like this man. He probably had become quite comfortable settling for second best. And the pool was familiar territory. We, too, find ourselves becoming comfortable in our less-than-ideal lifestyles. Jesus says to us as He did to the invalid, "Do you want to get well? Do you want to be all God desires you to be?"

Far too often our response is an excuse. "I'm yours as soon as I get out of high school. Later, Lord, when I'm in college, after I'm married, after children, after, after, later, later."

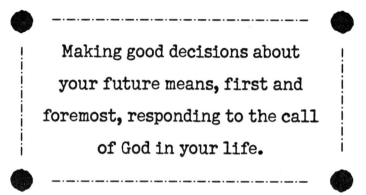

Making good decisions about your future means, first and foremost, responding to the call of God in your life.

Jesus says to us, though, "Get up! Pick up your mat and walk."

In other words, now is the time to respond to My call, He says. If you put it off you may never make the right decision. Making good decisions about your future means, first and foremost, responding to the call of God in your life.

When God whispers in a still, small voice in your mind, *Do you want to get well?* what aspect of your life is He talking about? Remember, the decisions you make today will affect you for eternity. Now is the time to respond.

What will it take for you to "go for it" in this life? What did the invalid in our story do?

The Sick Man Made a Conscious Decision to Get Well

Jesus asked him to pick up his mat and walk and the invalid *decided* to go for it. You can decide today to live life to the fullest. You can make a decision to "break the chain" and go for it. Dare to dream about the person you can become—and then dare to become the person of your dreams. Determination, patient perseverance and hard work mixed with faith in your Creator is what you need to make it happen.

John Erwin had skipped school too many times to count. He had stolen bicycles, ridden them to a junkyard and destroyed them. As a 12-year-old, John joined a gang of young toughs and threatened his foster parents with a 22-caliber rifle. A judge once said, "I don't know how any boy can be as mean as they say you are. But I'm convinced you'll never change. I predict you'll spend most of your life in institutions."

Three decades later the judge's prophecy had been partially fulfilled. In all, John Erwin had spent more than 25 years in a large, notorious institution—Chicago's Cook County Jail. But not as an inmate! The judge was mostly wrong; Erwin did change. Remarkably.

In the army, Erwin met a family who showed him the same love they had shown their own children. After a childhood of violence and sexual abuse, he experienced God's love and forgiveness.

He later founded PACE, one of America's most successful prison rehabilitation programs. He then joined the staff of Chuck Colson's Prison Fellowship. Erwin says, "I don't give up on people. If God can change me, He can change them too."[1]

John Erwin made a conscious decision to get well. He could have spent his days wasting his existence, wishing life had been more fair to him. He could have allowed his past failures to stop him, but he didn't. His life is a perfect illustration of someone who refused to settle for second best but developed a "go-for-it" attitude that literally changed history. He set his heart on a dream.

The Sick Man Was Set Free

Jesus made an exciting promise to everyone willing to listen: "You will know the truth, and the truth will set you free" (John 8:32). Far too many of your friends and maybe even your family will never really live liberated lives. You don't have to follow these negative patterns. You can choose to change. You can choose to take Jesus at His word and live life to the fullest.

Who do you want to be? What type of person do you want to become? In Christ, you can become that person. Here are 10 simple words that, if followed, will release you to go for it: *"I can do everything through him who gives me strength"* (Philippians 4:13).

Have you ever heard the Indian folk story about the little eagle who thought it was a prairie chicken?

> One day an Indian brave found an eagle's egg and put it into the nest of a prairie chicken. The eaglet hatched with the

brood of chicks and grew up with them. All its life the changeling eagle, thinking it was a prairie chicken, did what the prairie chickens did. It scratched in the dirt for seeds and insects to eat. It clucked and cackled. And it flew in a brief thrashing of wings and flurry of feathers no more than a few feet off the ground. After all, that's how prairie chickens fly.

Years passed, and the changeling eagle grew old. One day, the eagle saw a magnificent bird far above it in the cloudless sky. Hanging with graceful majesty on the powerful wind currents, it soared with scarcely a beat of its strong, golden wings. "What a beautiful bird!" said the changeling eagle to its neighbor. "What is it?"

"That's an eagle—the chief of the birds," the neighbor clucked. "But don't give it a second thought. You could never be like that bird."

So the changeling eagle never gave it another thought. And it died thinking it was a prairie chicken.

Being raised in a family of prairie chickens, this eagle began to think it *was* a prairie chicken and began to *act* like a prairie chicken. The changeling eagle spent its life looking up at the eagles and longing to join them among the clouds. But it never once occurred to the eagle to lift its wings and try to fly.

You have the ability to be an eagle, to soar above the rest of the crowd, to get over the hang-ups and peer pressure that bring you down. God calls you to break free from the crowd—free from the ball and chains that tie you down—and to soar with the eagles.

We make excuses. We say, "Lord, I don't live with prairie chickens, but I *am* being raised in a family of turkeys." And we *settle* for less than we were born to be.

It's my hope that you will be a person who is willing to break your chains, who is willing to say yes to Christ, who is willing to soar above the heights. That's not going to happen with excuses, nor will it happen by daydreaming. The only way it will happen is for you to invite Jesus to be Lord of your life and Lord of your ambitions. The Old Testament prophet Isaiah said:

Do you not know? Have you not heard? The Lord is the everlasting God, the Creator of the ends of the earth. He will not grow tired or weary, and his understanding no one can fathom. He gives strength to the weary and increases the power of the weak. Even youths grow tired and weary, and young men stumble and fall; but those who hope in the Lord will renew their strength. They will soar on wings like eagles; they will run and not grow weary, they will walk and not be faint (Isaiah 40:28-31).

I believe God plants a dream in every person's heart. Most of the time these dreams aren't grandiose. They are simple little ideas or desires to make this world a better place to live. What's your dream? What's your desire? Are you willing to make the important decisions today in order to ensure a wonderful tomorrow? Life is short...*Go for it!*

Developing a Positive Self-Image

If you are like most people, much of your life up to this point has been ruled by a weak self-image. None of us likes to admit the fact that we aren't perfect. So we hide behind a mask of either superiority or inferiority, trying to cover up the reality of our sense of failure.

We pursue popularity, power and success at the cost of compromising our true beliefs. Because we don't always like ourselves we struggle with loving and accepting others. We tend to gossip or compare ourselves, attempting to make ourselves more inferior or superior than our friends.

There are people who, on the outside, appear to have it all together but really, on the inside, they don't have a very good view of themselves either. These include:

- The boastful person;
- The insecure person;
- The driven-to-success person;
- The intimidated person;
- The critical/negative person;
- The materialistic person;
- The sexually promiscuous person.

One of the greatest tragedies of our day is that millions of people struggle with intense feelings of inferiority and a lack of self-worth. Without a healthy self-image, without the confidence that God is in us, on our side and pulling for us, we become fragile, easily bruised and counterproductive people.

If we're not careful, the inferiority cycle begins to take over our lives, and things just keep getting worse. The inferiority cycle begins with feelings of self-doubt, which, if they go unchecked, turn into self-hate. When we hate ourselves, we often express our feelings through negative and inappropriate behavior, keeping us on the downward spiral. The guilt about our actions causes more self-rejection, which in turn causes continued feelings of self-doubt.

When our self-esteem gets worse, we find our negative behavior becoming more destructive—and the spiral continues. In the end, we may resort to extremely negative escape hatches—drug and alcohol abuse, running away, sexual promiscuity, suicidal tendencies, aggression, anger—to ease the pain of our self-loathing.

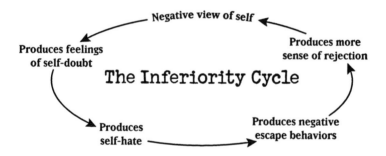

This book is about keeping the inferiority cycle from continuing. It really is possible to free yourself from many of the trappings of a negative self-image. You can't do it alone. You need God's help. You need the help of positive, supportive friends and family. You also need the desire to change. If you have the desire to be all God has intended you to be, then you are choosing to live your life on the cutting edge.

I love the story of Terry Foxe. He is truly one of my all-time heroes. Terry was a Canadian who, in order to raise money for cancer research, chose to run across Canada from the East Coast to Vancouver, British Columbia—more than 5,000 miles. Terry knew the needs of cancer victims intimately because his own body was filled with cancer. Every day he ran the equivalent of a 26-mile marathon across Canada on one leg. The other leg had already been amputated. During his heroic run, Terry's enthusiasm and zeal for life captured my interest, and I remember day after day seeing him on the news. He would usually be standing in front of a microphone in a park or shopping center or church building with people, mainly children, gathered around him. He would often say, "I don't know about tomorrow, but I'm thankful for today, and I'm going to make the most of this one day God has given me."

His thankful heart was an inspiration to millions of Canadians and people all around the world. Terry died before completing his run. He was only able to run 2,200 miles when he was taken back home to die. Before he died, he received the highest medal of honor from the Canadian government. By exhibiting a positive attitude, Terry knew how to take even horrible circumstances and turn them into victories.

Beauty, Brains and Bucks

Outstanding psychologist Dr. James Dobson says, "Beauty, intelligence and money are the three attributes valued most highly in our society."[1] I think he's exactly right. Because beauty, brains and bucks are so highly valued in our world, they tend to be major roadblocks to building a healthy self-esteem. In actuality, none of the "big three" attributes are evil or sinful, but when placed on an unreachable pedestal, they can be devastating to your self-image.

Beauty
I'm not going to tell you to quit brushing your teeth or using deodorant! I think you should do everything you can to look attractive. However, the pressure we all are under to pursue physical perfection is frightening, especially when you consider that about 80 percent of the teenagers in our society don't like the way they look![2]

The media has set unreasonable standards for physical appearance, making them unattainable for the vast majority of us. Yet millions of people strive to look like the latest rock stars, movie idols and sex symbols. Now hear this: *God does not place prime importance on physical appearance or strength.* Our society does. Our world is hung up on beauty and ability. You think I'm exaggerating? Who gets more attention in life, the pretty baby or the ugly one? Who gets more dates in high school, the beauty queen or the homely girl? Who was the student

body president at your local high school this year? The odds are, he or
she was a better-than-average-looking person.

For most of us, the inability to accept our physical appearance is
devastating to our self-esteem. The problems with our physical
appearance start very young. In my seventh-grade yearbook, Eddie
Hovdy wrote these words to me:

> God created rivers
> God created lakes
> God created you, Jim,
> Everyone makes mistakes.

I don't remember anything else about my seventh-grade yearbook, but those words are etched in my memory forever. To this day
I still remember reading that poem and putting my yearbook down,
trying to figure out why Eddie didn't like me. I thought about all the
physical characteristics I didn't like about myself. Eddie probably
didn't like me because of the split in my front teeth, my hairy legs or
my eyebrows. Besides, I was much shorter than Eddie. For days I was
depressed. I hated Eddie, but I also hated myself because I didn't
look as handsome as he did. Of course, Eddie probably wrote that
silly poem in everyone's yearbook, but you couldn't have convinced
me of this in the seventh grade.

Because physical appearance plays such an important role in our
self-esteem, it's extremely important to understand that God does not
look at your outside appearance. I'll never make it on the Mr. Universe
tour, so I take comfort in the conversation God has with the prophet
Samuel. God was talking to Samuel about a very handsome man whom
God was rejecting as a candidate for the next king of Israel. God said,
"Do not consider his appearance or his height, for I have rejected him.
The Lord does not look at the things man looks at. *Man looks at the
outward appearance, but the Lord looks at the heart*" (1 Samuel 16:7,
emphasis mine).

God simply places no importance on your physical appearance.
He focuses on your inner person. God's desire is that we have real
inner beauty. He wants you to recognize that He was active in your
very creation (see Psalm 139:13-15) and that He is still involved in
every part of your development.

Unfortunately, far too many people devote a great deal of time and attention to their outward appearance and not nearly enough to their inner beauty. You and I both know people who are stunningly beautiful on the outside and miserable on the inside. The most attractive people I know are those who have developed an inner beauty that radiates even to the outside, making them more physically beautiful as well.

Brains

When I was growing up there was a kid in our neighborhood named Tom, whom we nicknamed "Albert Fruitfly." We called him that because he was homely to look at and always in the slower classes in school. I'm ashamed to say I was one of the instigators of this horrible nickname. All throughout elementary, junior high and even into high school, we called him Albert Fruitfly.[3] We were all amazed that Tom graduated from high school, but he did. He immediately moved from our city, and I lost track of him completely.

Out of the clear blue, nine years after high school, Tom called me to say he was coming to town on business and wanted to take me to lunch. We agreed on a time and a restaurant. I got to the restaurant first. A very attractive executive, who radiated confidence and intelligence, walked over to me, stuck out his hand and greeted me. I would never, ever have recognized him! When we sat down, I asked Tom to tell me his story.

He told me that all his life his parents had compared him with his older brother, who always received straight *A*'s. Tom just assumed he was dumb and ugly, because that's what everyone told him. When he graduated from high school, he moved to another part of California. He attended a junior college and, without the negative influences, earned great grades. He started attending a Christian club on campus and eventually made a commitment to Jesus Christ. Tom learned that, in God's eyes, he wasn't dumb *or* ugly. God believed in him even when he didn't believe in himself. Tom attended university, then went on to get his M.B.A. He married a beautiful woman and had two great kids.

I left that lunch with two very different emotions. I was absolutely ecstatic that Tom had become such a fulfilled person. If Tom could do it, with God's help anyone could. I also felt a deep sense of shame for taking an active part in making his early years unhappy. Please never forget God's idea of intelligence is very different from the world's.

Bucks

A popular bumper sticker reads, "The person with the most toys wins." What a lie. More toys, more money, more things do not bring happiness. In fact, they usually bring more emptiness. I'm not suggesting you should live in a cave. However, I strongly challenge you to examine whether you are building your esteem upon material wealth. If you are, then get ready for disappointment in the future.

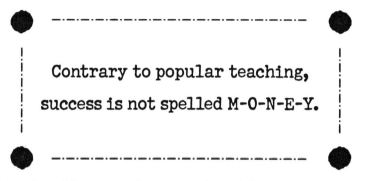

Contrary to popular teaching, success is not spelled M-O-N-E-Y.

Material wealth seems to be everyone's goal these days, and many have "sold their souls" for the almighty dollar—lying, cheating and stealing to get to the top financially. Contrary to popular teaching, success is not spelled M-O-N-E-Y.

A few years ago, I decided to tackle the subject of money and stewardship with our youth group at church. Honestly, I had no idea what to expect. I started out with a simple discussion starter. "Let's go around the living room and share what we want to be when we grow up."

Derrick was first. He said, "I want to be rich."

"Okay," I replied, "but what do you want to do to become rich?"

He shot back, "I don't really care what I do; I just want to make a lot of money, live by the ocean and drive a Porsche."

At first I thought Derrick was kidding, but I seemed to be the only one in our group amused by his comment. All the other students took his statement at face value.

Another young man in the group said he wanted to be an entrepreneur. Again I laughed, but he was serious. When I was in high school, I didn't even know what an entrepreneur was, and I still can't spell the word without the help of a dictionary.

Now I'm not opposed to money or even the necessary pursuit of money, but Derrick and some of the others in the group were expecting materialism to bring happiness. They had bought into the lie that if you wear the right clothes, drive the perfect car, purchase the best of whatever, then you will be truly happy.

Jesus had some insightful words to say about material wealth.

> "Do not store up for yourselves treasures on earth, where moth and rust destroy, and where thieves break in and steal. But store up for yourselves treasures in heaven, where moth and rust do not destroy, and where thieves do not break in and steal. For where your treasure is, there your heart will be also" (Matthew 6:19-21).

Recently I heard a man tell us in our church, "I spent my life climbing the ladder of success. When I got to the top I owned a million-dollar house, a boat, cars and enough money to do anything I wanted. But I had lost my family, friends, my self-esteem and my faith in God. I realized I'd wasted my life climbing the wrong ladder."

Finances are not a peripheral issue in our faith. Jesus spent more time talking about money than He did about love. Jesus was talking about faith and commitment when He said, "For where your treasure is, there your heart will be also."

Materialism will take you down the wrong road. In 1923, a meeting was held at the Edgewater Beach Hotel in Chicago. Attending this meeting were nine of the world's most successful financiers: Charles Schwab, steel magnate; Samuel Insull, president of the largest utility company; Howard Hopson, president of the largest gas company; Arthur Cotton, the greatest wheat speculator; Richard Whitney, president of the New York Stock Exchange; Albert Fall, a member of the President's Cabinet; Leon Fraser, president of the Bank of International Settlements; Jesse Livermore, the great "bear" on Wall Street; and Ivar Krueger, head of the most powerful monopoly.

Twenty-five years later, things were different. Charles Schwab had died in bankruptcy, having lived on borrowed money for five years before his death. Samuel Insull had died a fugitive from justice, penniless in a foreign land. Howard Hopson was insane. Arthur Cotton had died abroad, insolvent. Richard Whitney had spent time in Sing Sing. Albert Fall had been pardoned so that he could die at home. Jesse Livermore, Ivar Krueger and Leon Fraser had all died by suicide. All of these men had learned well the art of making a living, but none of them had learned how to *live!*[4]

The words of Jesus make a lot of sense. "No one can serve two masters. Either he will hate the one and love the other, or he will be devoted to the one and despise the other. You cannot serve both God and Money" (Matthew 6:24).

My Name Is "I Am"

Developing a positive self-image is a lifelong process. You won't wake up one morning and say, "I think I'll have it all together for the rest of my life." Obviously, it doesn't work that way. The earlier you can build a healthy foundation for growth in your life—and the less entangled you become in the lies of the world—the happier you will be. You can't fret about your past, and worrying about the future will only tie you in knots. I often refer back to this poem, which was written with a good perspective on the big picture:

I AM

I was regretting the past
And fearing the future...
Suddenly my Lord was speaking:
"MY NAME IS I AM." He paused.
I waited. He continued,

"WHEN YOU LIVE IN THE PAST,
WITH ITS MISTAKES AND REGRETS,
IT IS HARD. I AM NOT THERE.
MY NAME IS NOT I WAS."

"WHEN YOU LIVE IN THE FUTURE,
WITH ITS PROBLEMS AND FEARS,
IT IS HARD. I AM NOT THERE.
MY NAME IS NOT I WILL BE."

"WHEN YOU LIVE IN THIS MOMENT,
IT IS NOT HARD.
I AM HERE.
MY NAME IS I AM."

—Helen Mallicoat[5]

Here's a little questionnaire to help you see just where you need work in your self-image.[6]

	Most of the time	Some-times	Hardly ever
1. Are you a critical person?	_____	_____	_____
2. Are you a poor listener?	_____	_____	_____
3. Are you argumentative with friends or family?	_____	_____	_____
4. Would you consider yourself an angry person?	_____	_____	_____
5. Are you a forgiving person?	_____	_____	_____
6. Are you very impressed with titles, honors or degrees?	_____	_____	_____
7. Do you have difficulty accepting compliments from others?	_____	_____	_____
8. Do the people who know you consider you overly sensitive?	_____	_____	_____
9. Do you always have to be right?	_____	_____	_____
10. Are you a jealous person?	_____	_____	_____
11. Do you find it difficult to lose in games and sports or any other events?	_____	_____	_____

Everyone has traits that need to be worked on. Using the questionnaire as a guide, list three areas in which you need the most improvement and three areas in which you are doing well. What can you do to begin working on your more difficult areas?

Peer Pressure
and Self-Esteem

You and I have an incredibly strong need to be loved and accepted by our friends and family. Actually, the drive to be liked is so strong we will do almost anything to be accepted by a peer group. Peer pressure will be the driving force behind many of the most difficult struggles in your life.

What *power* causes a 16-year-old girl named Janet to "go all the way" sexually when it goes against the way she was brought up—when she knows better? What power causes Tom at age 14 to drink a six-pack of beer with some new "friends," steal his family's car and go for a joyride? He didn't like the taste of alcohol; he was scared to death he would get caught with the car. He didn't even really like the guys with whom he was drinking. What power, what pressure causes people to do things they really don't want to do? Peer pressure.

Janet came to a new school. She wanted to be in the most popular group, but she wasn't. She didn't like her looks. When she played the comparison game, she lost. So she started to hang around with a somewhat wilder group than she was used to and went to one of their parties. Janet got drunk, but didn't realize how drunk. After a few more drinks, she was not in control of her emotions, and her decision-making process was blurred. A guy she really liked came up to her and started flirting. They started kissing, and he convinced her to go to a back bedroom. Janet wanted to be liked by this guy so much that she allowed him to have sex with her. It was her first time. Today, Janet is six months pregnant.

Tom wanted to be accepted by a group of neighborhood guys who were a few years older. He didn't want to be known as the goody-goody Christian kid. He drank too much, took his parents' car and, with his "friends" in the car, crashed the car in downtown San Clemente, California. Fortunately, even though the car was totaled, no one was critically injured. This time they were lucky.

Make no mistake about it, peer pressure is extremely powerful. The pressure to compromise and conform in order to belong and be accepted will force you to make some very tough decisions.

The apostle Paul summarized some of his deepest feelings with these words:

> I don't understand myself at all, for I really want to do what is right, but I can't. I do what I don't want to—what I hate. I know perfectly well that what I am doing is wrong, and my bad conscience proves that I agree with these laws I am breaking. But I can't help myself, because I'm no longer doing it. It is sin inside me that is stronger than I am that makes me do these evil things.
>
> I know I am rotten through and through so far as my old sinful nature is concerned. No matter which way I turn I can't make myself do right. I want to but I can't. When I want to do good, I don't; and when I try not to do wrong, I do it anyway. Now if I am doing what I don't want to, it is plain where the trouble is: sin still has me in its evil grasp.
>
> It seems to be a fact of life that when I want to do what is right, I inevitably do what is wrong. I love to do God's will so far as my new nature is concerned; but there is something else deep within me, in my lower nature, that is at war with my mind and wins the fight and makes me a slave to the sin that is still within me. In my mind I want to be God's willing servant but instead I find myself still enslaved to sin.
>
> So you see how it is: my new life tells me to do right, but the old nature that is still inside me loves to sin. Oh, what a terrible predicament I'm in! Who will free me

from my slavery to this deadly lower nature? Thank God!
It has been done by Jesus Christ our Lord. He has set me
free (Romans 7:15-25, *TLB*).

The battle against peer pressure is one you will fight the rest of
your life. It will never be easy to overcome the urge to compromise
your true values to be accepted by the group. Adults struggle with
peer pressure every day. I guess what I'm trying to say is this: Peer
pressure is not something you will grow out of as you get older.

However, as you discover your self-esteem rooted in God's love,
you can win this battle. Just because you will have to face peer pressure the rest of your life does not mean you can't have victory over
it. Negative peer influence is a foe you can defeat.

Don't Underestimate the Influence of Your Friends

I'll discuss this important principle in more detail in chapter seven,
but for now remember this: It's a fact that you become like your
friends. Think for a moment about your two or three best friends.
Now, consider how many things you have in common with one
another. You tend to dress in a similar style, listen to the same kind
of music and enjoy the same activities and interests.

Even though you may not want to hear the truth, it is this: If your
closest friends experiment with drugs, the odds are very strong that
you will, too. If your friends are sexually promiscuous, you will eventually turn in that direction. We become like the people we hang
around with and who influence us.

A 14-year-old guy once asked me, "What's so important about my
friends anyway?"

"You tell me," I replied.

He went to a chalkboard and wrote the following impressions:

My friends influence me on:
What I think about myself.
What language I use.
What I think of my parents.
What I wear.

What's *in* and what's not *in*.
What I think about my teachers.
How I act.
What parties I attend.
Whether studies are important.
Whether or not to drink or smoke.
What is right or wrong.
Whether or not to have team spirit.
Whether I should keep going to church.
How I should spend my money.
What I want to do when I graduate from high school.

After he had listed those 15 of his own answers, I looked at him and said, "I think you answered your own question."

Now let me ask you a question. Do your friends pull you up and build your self-image, or do they hold you down and, in reality, hurt your self-image? Only you can answer that question honestly in your heart of hearts. But don't underestimate the influence of your friends.

Dare to Be Different

You are unique and very special in God's eyes. You can dare to be different because you are loved and accepted by the One who matters

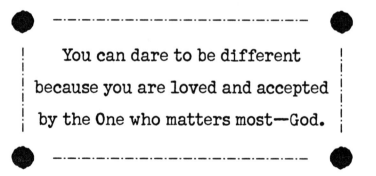

You can dare to be different because you are loved and accepted by the One who matters most—God.

most—God. I like the way a man named J. B. Phillips translated a verse in the book of Romans, where it says, "Don't let the world around you *squeeze* you into its own mold, but let God remold your minds from within, so that you may prove in practice that the plan of God for you is good, meets all his demands and moves toward the goal of true maturity" (12:2, italics mine).

Robert was in my youth group. He was normal and had his share of problems, but somehow he usually managed to rise above the negative influence of peer pressure. I asked him what his secret was, and he gave me an excellent formula I now pass on to you. Robert called this his "Will You Care or Remember?" inventory test. Here's how it works.

He wrote these words on a piece of paper:

> Ten years after I've left my school, will I still care about or be able to remember:
> * The girl or guy who was better dressed than I?
> * The number one athlete in the school?
> * The beauty queen or handsomest guy?
> * The person with the most expensive car?
> * The names of five people in a clique who wouldn't accept me in the group?
> * Who was or wasn't at the wildest parties?

What will really matter 10 years from now? If you are honest with yourself, you will realize that a lot of things you worry about when it comes to peer acceptance won't even matter a few years from now.

Today, God gave you 24 hours to live life to the fullest. That's 1,400 minutes or 86,400 seconds. You can accomplish a great deal with 1,440 minutes in a day. I hope you will take a life inventory today and decide not to follow the crowd, but dare to be different.

Once, when I was in eighth grade, we were having a slumber party at my home. It was 2:30 in the morning and we were still going strong. My parents had given up on us going to bed for the night. As guys often do at these kinds of parties, we started playing a game called "I Dare You." Basically, it was a game of peer pressure, and we were doing really weird things to be accepted by our group.

I only remember a few of the dares, but they were things such as "climb a tree in the backyard" and "knock on the neighbor's door." (Our poor neighbors!) My friend John Garrett had to put his boxers on his head and run around the yard. Like I said, they were just silly, weird dares. When it was my turn, the group dared me to go two doors down from our house to the supermarket parking lot and buy a newspaper. By this time it was 3:30 in the morning. Because I wanted to be accepted, I said I would do it.

Dressed only in boxers[1] (what else do eighth-grade guys wear at a slumber party?) and my heart pounding, I sprinted to the supermarket and put a quarter in the newspaper machine. I happened to look next door at the Winchell's Donut Shop. Who hangs out at donut shops at 3:30 in the morning? If you guessed police, you're right. A police officer was eating a donut and drinking coffee just 25 feet away from me. All of a sudden our eyes met. His light went on and I was caught. Not only was I feeling like a criminal, but in my boxers I felt like a pervert.

He questioned me, and I told him about the "I Dare You" game and that I lived around the corner. He put me in his patrol car and took me home. By this time, my friends, who had been hiding behind the supermarket in *their* boxers, were all back at my house in their sleeping bags quietly pretending to be asleep. At 3:30 A.M. the police officer, carrying his donut, knocked loudly on our front door. My father heard the knock at the door and was angry because he thought it was my fun-loving group. He stomped to the door, turned on the light and scowled at us—but for only a moment. Then it registered with him that his youngest son was standing next to an officer of the law. He looked at the officer and then at me in my boxers. The truly funny thing was that as the police officer started to describe what had just taken place, the officer started to laugh. You see, my father was also standing at the door in *his* boxers.

I look back at that experience and laugh because we will do almost anything for acceptance.

Handling Your Emotions:
Am I Normal?

I recently asked a small group of junior and senior high school students to choose the most difficult emotions for teenagers from the list below:

Worry	Moodiness
Stress	Loneliness
Fear	Depression
Anxiety	Anger
Guilt	Passion

A very sharp tenth grader raised her hand and said, "You just listed my autobiography." We all laughed, but the more we talked the more we realized that, for many people, the teenage years are filled with intense emotions that can often seem out of control. When our emotions are out of control, one of the symptoms is low self-esteem.

Let's face it, we live in a fast-paced, pressure-filled society in which it's a full-time struggle just to keep up. While you're making the transition from the carefree days of childhood to the breakneck pace of modern adulthood, you will be dealing with the normal "growing pains" of adolescence—social stress, body stress, school stress, parent stress, sexual stress, peer pressure stress, religion stress and all the rest. There is the very real potential for you to snap under all that pressure.

Pressure comes from every direction. I don't remember where I came across these lines concerning what teenagers worry about, but I like them. Teenagers worry:

- That in a long kiss, you'll have to breathe through your nose and your nose will be stopped up;
- That your breath smells;
- That you have B.O.;
- That if you are a girl, you won't have breasts;
- That if you are a boy, you *will* have breasts;
- That if you are a boy, you'll never be able to grow a mustache;
- That if you are a girl, you *will* have a mustache;
- That when you go to the bathroom, people will hear;
- That the lock on the bathroom door doesn't work, or that someone will walk in.

Like most people, there are times when you are both depressed and totally happy in the same day. I think it's possible to be consumed with the anxiety of a broken relationship and, in the very next minute, feel completely at peace. You can feel a real sense of guilt about a very small infraction, or your conscience may not even be stirred when you really compromise your convictions in a big way.

Emotions are strange creatures. Just when you think you have tamed a certain emotion, it flares up worse than ever. Is it possible to trust your feelings and emotions? Why do you act the way you do? Are you normal or a little crazy? If these are your questions, welcome to the teenage years. *Nobody said it would be easy!*

Your emotions play an important part in how you feel about life. This chapter is not meant to be an in-depth psychological look at teenage emotions, but rather a practical guide to help you through the tough times.

A majority of people seem to believe (or want to believe) that there is a world this side of heaven where we will be problem free and pain free; a world with intimate relationships yet no conflict with others or ourselves; a world where we are always in tune with God. Unfortunately, that world does not exist on this side of heaven. The opening sentence in one of this century's best-selling books, *The Road Less Traveled,* is: "Life is difficult." Friend, life isn't always fair. In each and every one of our lives there will be difficult times.

Jesus concluded the greatest sermon ever preached with this illustration:

> "Therefore everyone who hears these words of mine and puts them into practice is like a wise man who built his house on the rock. The rain came down, the streams rose, and the winds blew and beat against that house; yet it did not fall, because it had its foundation on the rock. But everyone who hears these words of mine and does not put them into practice is like a foolish man who built his house on sand. The rain came down, the streams rose, and the winds blew and beat against that house, and it fell with a great crash" (Matthew 7:24-27).

This story reminds us that rain, wind and storms come to everyone. No one is exempt from tough times. How we *prepare* for the storms of life makes all the difference in the world. What you do with your foundation is your choice. You can build your life on the Rock— or gamble on the sand.

Five Important Principles

Here are five principles for you to follow to keep your life from crumbling under the pressure:

- Stay healthy;
- Develop meaningful relationships;
- Avoid negativism;
- Reach out to others;
- Live one day at a time.

Stay Healthy

People who aren't healthy are usually very unhappy. To combat intense negative emotions, it's important to watch what you eat, keep your body in good physical shape, get plenty of sleep and set aside enough time for relaxation. How are you doing in each of these areas?

If just one of these is out of kilter, you can't be living life to the fullest.

When you improve your physical life, you will feel more in control of the other parts of your life as well. When I'm tired, I am grumpy. When I've driven my body to the point of exhaustion, I am more likely to experience such emotions as anger, depression and worry. God made our bodies to function together with our minds and spirits. Odds are that if you are not taking care of your body, the other areas of your life are also in lousy shape.

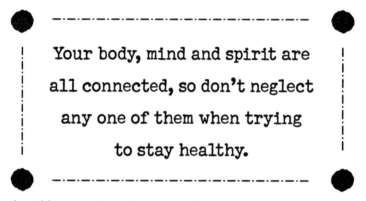

Your body, mind and spirit are all connected, so don't neglect any one of them when trying to stay healthy.

The Bible reminds us why we need to keep our bodies healthy. "Do you not know that your body is a temple of the Holy Spirit, who is in you, whom you have received from God? You are not your own; you were bought at a price. Therefore honor God with your body" (1 Corinthians 6:19,20).

If you are experiencing intense negative emotions, then by all means get a physical checkup. You may be dealing with a correctable physical problem that needs medical attention. I know a young woman who was experiencing extreme moodiness and severe depression. She tried everything to pull herself out of her despair. Finally she visited her doctor and found that she had, along with an irregular and painful menstruation cycle, a hormone imbalance. The doctor prescribed treatment that corrected the physical problem, and the emotional problems went away also.

To stay healthy you must also keep your mind and thought patterns healthy. Counseling is a positive option for anyone who is struggling with negative thoughts. When I was in graduate school and studied counseling, it was mandatory for those of us in the program to receive counseling. At first I didn't want to go. After all, I wasn't crazy. When I did end up having eight counseling sessions, I can honestly say that those sessions with a counselor were some of the most freeing times I'd ever experienced. Your body, mind and spirit are all connected, so don't neglect any one of them when trying to stay healthy.

Develop Meaningful Relationships

Spend time with positive, uplifting people. We all need to risk attaining more intimate relationships. Most of us have too many people we can call acquaintances and not enough people we can call intimate friends. Kristi was a song leader, an outstanding swimmer and very active in my church youth group. One day she called me and blurted out, "Jim, I don't have any friends. No one likes me. No one knows me."

Kristi totally threw me a curve. I assumed that because she was active she had plenty of intimate friends with whom she could share her hurts, dreams and joys. She said, "No one ever calls me so I sit at home when everybody else is out doing something."

As we investigated this problem together, we found out that others assumed Kristi was already busy, so they didn't bother to call. We also learned that Kristi needed to initiate relationships with others. When she made the calls and planned to do things with others, they were sincerely excited to spend time with her.

Perhaps the smartest move Kristi made was to launch a weekly support group with three other girls from our church. It wasn't part of the church program. They made it happen. Those four girls became the best of friends, and their weekly meetings continued throughout high school. Kristi graduated from high school happier and healthier because she took the risk and developed meaningful relationships.

Avoid Negativism

People who are negative, critical, argumentative and self-condemning are unhappy people. Negative thinking is simply a bad habit. Did you know it can take as little as three weeks to form a lifelong habit? The good news is you can also eliminate some of your bad habits in just three weeks. It takes work, but it's worth it.

Here's what helps me: *Thank therapy.* I make it a point each day to decide whether I'm going to be a person who grumbles and complains my way through life, or to be a person who is thankful and grateful. It's really up to me.

The Bible says, "No matter what happens, always be thankful, for this is God's will for you who belong to Christ Jesus" (1 Thessalonians

5:18, *TLB*). The *New International Version* urges us to "give thanks in all circumstances."

Notice that Scripture does not say to be thankful *for* all situations; it says to be thankful *in* all situations. How ridiculous it seems to be thankful for a difficult problem! But when we are challenged to be thankful *in* all circumstances, it is much easier to see that even in difficult times there are reasons to be thankful.

At one time or another, everyone begins to feel sorry for himself or herself. At times we feel we "got the short end of the stick." Yet it is important for us to have an attitude of thankfulness. No matter

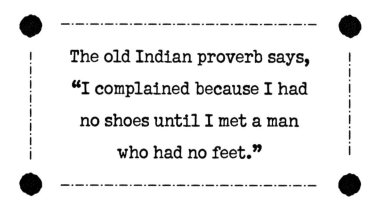

The old Indian proverb says, "I complained because I had no shoes until I met a man who had no feet."

who you are or what troubles have come your way, you have a great many reasons to be thankful. Sometimes we need to be reminded of the old Indian proverb that says, "I complained because I had no shoes until I met a man who had no feet."

You can avoid negativism and practice thankfulness. For me, *thank therapy* means focusing on reasons why I am thankful. I tend to have tunnel vision and forget the many, many reasons I have to be grateful. Try this: When you are feeling negative, list on a piece of paper all the reasons you can think of why you are thankful. As you become consciously aware of why you are thankful, you can't help but be less critical and negative. Practice makes perfect, so perhaps it's time to put this book down and make thankfulness a habit.

Reach Out to Others

There are two kinds of people in the world: self-absorbed, "me first," I-centered people and those who are others-centered. Think for a moment about the happiest people you know. They are probably the most others-centered people you know. If you want to be happy, become a person who reaches out to others.

1. Do favors for your friends and family.
2. Give compliments.
3. Be available to serve.
4. Remember that listening is the language of love.

If you are unhappy, take a serious look at just how much of your life revolves around *you*. Self-centered people will always struggle with feelings of inferiority. I heard a story of a woman who was negative, critical, sick and deeply depressed. She had gone from one medical doctor to another looking for a cure. Each time the doctors would run extensive tests and find nothing physically wrong. She finally visited a very wise, old physician. Instead of just checking her physically, he listened to what he called her "me focus." He sensed she needed to quit looking inward and begin to reach out.

When he finished the checkup, he asked her to come into his office. There he handed her a prescription. It read: *Do something nice for someone else for 14 days in a row, then come back and see me.*

She said, "That's it?"

He smiled and said, "That's it. You try this prescription, and I think you will feel 100 percent better."

Well, she did do something nice for someone else every day for two weeks. Her gifts of service weren't earth shattering. They were more along the line of baking cookies for a lonely elderly woman in her neighborhood, and actually taking the time to listen to a hurting friend. For two weeks she took joy in doing special little acts of love for others. She then realized the doctor was right. She felt better than she could ever remember feeling. Maybe we can learn a lesson from this story.

Live One Day at a Time

Jesus gave us some important advice when He said, "Do not worry about tomorrow, for tomorrow will worry about itself. Each day has enough trouble of its own" (Matthew 6:34). In other words, live one day at a time. Did you know that:

85 percent of our worries will never happen?

10 percent of our worries will happen whether we worry
or not?

5 percent of our worries are valid?

I know a man who lived his life by this formula: "If each day is lived as it comes, each task is done as it appears, then the sum of your days will be good." He died a happy and fulfilled man.

You can live your life on purpose. Stop living accidentally, letting the winds of change carry you from crisis to crisis. Stop letting circumstances rule your emotions and determine your outlook on life. You can *choose* to be happy. You can even choose happiness in the midst of pain. Abraham Lincoln once said, "Most people are about as happy as they choose to be."

It's time to quit blaming your unhappiness on others or on your circumstances. Take responsibility for your own happiness.

Life is too short to focus on the mundane rather than on the miraculous.

Life is too short to hold a grudge.

Life is too short to keep your room perfect.

Life is too short to let a day pass without hugging a loved one.

Life is too short to put off Bible study and prayer—to stay indoors—or settle for second best in life.

Life is too short, way too short, to choose mediocrity.

If you want to prepare yourself for the emotional storms of life that come your way, you have to start small. Set specific goals that will stretch you, but are attainable. Experience little successes along the way. Growth requires effort. Even if you don't *feel* like it, do it anyway. Your feelings will often follow your actions. Never, never forget that God believes in you, wants the best for you and is willing to walk with you through your most difficult times.

Here's a prayer that has been helpful to me. It's called the Serenity Prayer:

God grant me the serenity
to accept the things I cannot change,
the courage to change the things I can,
and the wisdom to know the difference.
—St. Francis of Assisi

6

Good News for Imperfect People

A few years back, I heard a story about a distinguished man dressed in a three-piece business suit who caused quite an uproar in downtown Chicago. One bright, busy morning, with thousands of people going about their business on Michigan Avenue, this nicely dressed gentleman stood on a street corner, pointed his finger at another man and shouted, *"Guilty!"* People standing around assumed these two men knew each other. They didn't. The first man walked around the corner, pointed at another stranger and again screamed at the top of his voice, *"Guilty!"*

For more than three hours, this distinguished-looking man walked Michigan Avenue. He would stop, turn, point and shout, *"Guilty!"* At first people thought he was crazy. Literally hundreds of people began following him, watching him. Some thought maybe he had some kind of spiritual insight because everyone he pointed to *was* guilty. "How did he know?" they began to ask. Was he a prophet? Finally, just as quickly as he had appeared, he left and was never heard from again.

Why all the commotion about this guy? Possibly because at the core of every human being there is a sense of guilt. We all feel we've missed the mark—and we're right. The Bible puts the bad news this way: "For all have sinned and fall short of the glory of God" (Romans 3:23).

The Bible also tells us the price of sin is death, or spiritual separation from God. The verb "to sin" means literally to miss the mark.

If you think of a target and what happens when the arrow misses the bull's-eye, then you understand what it means to miss the mark. God is perfect; we are not. Because we are not perfect, we miss the mark set by God's righteousness. That's why we feel guilty, and that's bad news.

The way I best remember the term "to miss the mark" is one of my more embarrassing stories. Cathy and I had become what our friends

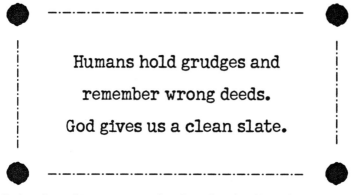

Humans hold grudges and remember wrong deeds. God gives us a clean slate.

called an "item." We were now boyfriend and girlfriend. I had not yet kissed her, but every night for months I had practiced kissing her on my pillow. (I don't believe I'm actually telling this story!) Each night I would close my eyes, tilt my head and imagine kissing Cathy on the lips. The night came when I had this special feeling that I would actually get to kiss the real thing instead of the pillow. We had gone to a Christmas party and, when I walked her to her dorm door, somehow I knew this was the moment I had been waiting for. I closed my eyes, tilted my head and, the next thing I knew, I felt something strange on my lips. I opened my eyes to see that I had missed her lips and kissed her right nostril! I drove home that night screaming in my car, "I missed her lips! I missed her lips!"

Okay, I think you get the picture on missing the mark. Now for the good news. There is hope for those who aren't perfect! We do not need to remain guilty of missing the mark. In Christ, we can be set free from our sin. That's great news! Let me explain.

God's ways are different from ours. Many people who have good intentions have some real misconceptions when it comes to their view of God. Some think God is a god of works. They think we must *earn* His love the way we earn grades in school. They're wrong. Our God is the God of grace. Grace means unmerited favor. In other words, you didn't have to do anything to receive His love. The New Testament puts it this way: "For it is by grace you have been saved, through faith—and this not from yourselves, it is the gift of God—not by works, so that no one can boast" (Ephesians 2:8,9).

Others think God is slow to forgive. Maybe they live in a family where people hold grudges. But God's forgiveness is ours for the asking. Humans hold grudges and remember wrong deeds. God actually forgets confessed sin. We are the ones who keep bringing up the past. God gives us a clean slate. I like what a pastor said about forgiveness: "You have no right to dredge up anything that God has forgiven and forgotten. He has put it behind His back."[1]

God's ways are different from ours, and if we are ever going to establish a positive sense of self-worth, we must learn His ways.

God Loves You Unconditionally

You are loved, not for what you do, but for who you are. If you're anything like me, you believe, you doubt, you get discouraged, you fight with those you love, you compromise your actions to be accepted, you justify your shortcomings, you go against God's best for you, and yet *God loves you for who you are.*

To be set free you must come to believe that God loves you as you are and not as you should be. When one of my precious daughters would skin her knee as a youngster, I didn't yell, "You stupid kid! You are the dumbest child in all of California." I would pick her up and reassure her that everyone stumbles and falls as they learn to walk—and run.

The unconditional love of God is expressed beautifully in this story about a woman caught in sexual sin:

> Jesus went to the Mount of Olives. At dawn he appeared again in the temple courts, where all the people gathered around him, and he sat down to teach them. The teachers of the law and the Pharisees brought in a woman caught in adultery. They made her stand before the group and said to Jesus, "Teacher, this woman was caught in the act of adultery. In the Law Moses commanded us to stone such women. Now what do you say?" They were using this question as a trap, in order to have a basis for accusing him.

But Jesus bent down and started to write on the ground with his finger. When they kept on questioning him, he straightened up and said to them, "If any one of you is without sin, let him be the first to throw a stone at her." Again he stooped down and wrote on the ground.

At this, those who heard began to go away one at a time, the older ones first, until only Jesus was left, with the woman still standing there. Jesus straightened up and asked her, "Woman, where are they? Has no one condemned you?"

"No one, sir," she said.

"Then neither do I condemn you," Jesus declared. "Go now and leave your life of sin" (John 8:1-11).

What a story! Picture for a moment all those men holding rocks in their hands ready to stone this woman to death for being caught in the very act of committing adultery. (I've always wondered what happened to the man in this story.) What did they think Jesus would say? After all, the Law of Moses gave them the right to kill her. Jesus simply looked in their condescending eyes and said, "If any one of you is without sin, let him be the first to throw a stone at her."

Knowing full well that they, too, had missed the mark of God's righteousness, they all turned around and left. Christ's point was made loud and clear.

In this story, we hear an intimate conversation between a woman who had missed the mark and the Lord who had every right to kill her. Showing deep compassion and unconditional love, He asked her where were the ones who accused her. She probably looked around just to make sure and said, "No one is left, sir."

Jesus then showed the world the true character of God's love when He said, "Then neither do I condemn you."

Did Jesus say her sin was okay? Not at all. In fact, He told her to leave her life of sin. But the words "neither do I condemn you" are the same words He says to Christians even now. He loves you completely and unconditionally.

Once upon a time there was a young girl named Susie. She was a beautiful little girl with the most wonderful doll collection. Her father traveled all over the world on business, and for nearly 12 years he had brought dolls home to Susie. In her bedroom, she had shelves full of dolls from across the United States and around the world. She had dolls who could sing, dolls who could dance—dolls who could do just about anything a doll could possibly do.

One day one of her father's business acquaintances came to dinner. After the meal, he asked Susie about her doll collection. Susie took him by the hand and showed him her marvelous dolls from around the world. He was very impressed. After he took the "grand tour" and was personally introduced to many of the beautiful dolls, he

> **God loves you, not for what you do, but for who you are. He loves you because you are His special creation.**

asked Susie, "Of all these precious dolls you must have one that is your favorite. Which one is it?"

Without a moment's hesitation, Susie went over to an old, beat-up toy box and started pulling out toys. From the bottom of the box she pulled one of the most ragged stuffed dolls the man had ever seen. Only a few strands of hair were left on her head. Her clothing had long since disappeared. The doll was filthy from many years of play outside. One of the button eyes was hanging down, with only a string to keep it attached. Stuffing was coming out at the elbow and knee. Susie handed the doll to the gentleman and said, "This doll is my favorite."

The man, visibly shocked, asked, "Why this old doll when you have all these beautiful dolls in your room?"

She replied, "If I didn't love this doll, nobody would!"

The businessman was moved to tears. It was such a simple statement, yet so profound. The little girl loved that doll unconditionally. She loved the doll, not for its beauty or abilities, but simply because it was her very own doll.

God loves you the way Susie loved her doll. God loves you, not for what you do, but for who you are. You never need to earn God's love. He loves you because you are His special creation. Because of God's unconditional love, you are free to blossom into all He wants you to be. His love has no strings attached.

God's Love Is Sacrificial

Here is a fact that must be forever placed in our minds. "God demonstrates his own love for us in this: While we were still sinners, Christ died for us" (Romans 5:8).

If you ever doubt God's love for you, then look to the Cross. I am convinced that if you were the only person ever born into this world, Christ still would have sacrificed His life for you so that you could have a relationship with God.

Sometimes I need to be reminded of the actual physical pain and the undeniable humiliation He went through for people who really don't take Him all that seriously. His sacrifice on the cross is the very reason we can have a positive self-worth. Because we all have missed the mark, none of us can honestly look at ourselves and feel *really* good. Self-esteem, however, is available to us because it is rooted in the sacrificial love of God.

I like most people. However, I didn't like Clark (not his real name). A few years ago, six-year-old Clark lived in our neighborhood. He declared he wanted to marry our daughter Christy, who was also six at the time. Clark had a horrible mouth, and was a bad influence on our girls. One summer day, Clark was out in the middle of the street as I was driving home from work. I honked my horn to get him to move out of the road, and he flipped me the international sign of displeasure! I think you get the picture.

Now let me tell you about a dream I had, in which Clark and my three girls, Christy, Rebecca and Heidi, are playing with a beach ball in our front yard. Clark is being his typical ornery self. I'm watching from the front porch. The ball goes out into the street, and my girls go after the ball. At the same time, I see a huge truck racing around the corner.

There is no way the truck can stop in time. Without a moment's hesitation I rush to the street. I smell the burning rubber of tires skidding. I push the girls aside, and, just before I get crushed, I wake up. Whew!

I know that I would sacrifice my life for my children. After all, I love them and have a principal role in molding the women they will become. Now, back to my dream. Again, I watch Clark and the girls play with the beach ball. This time when the ball goes into the street and the truck races around the corner, Clark starts to run toward the ball. He is going to get crushed and I...stop. I hesitate, and then I wake up. (Clark is still hanging around, so I'm sure it's just a dream.) I'm not sure I would have given my life for Clark.

God showed us how much He loved us even while we turned our backs on Him. Jesus suffered and died on the cross. Now *that's* what I call sacrificial love.

God Created You in His Image

I like this verse: "For we are God's workmanship, created in Christ Jesus to do good works" (Ephesians 2:10). You are God's workmanship. The New Testament was written in the Greek language, and the word for "workmanship" can also be translated as "poetry." You are a "poem of God." How does it feel to know you are the handiwork of God?

You are His workmanship.

You are His poetry.

You are special.

You are gifted.

You are unique.

You are different from any other person in the world.

Because you were created in His image, you can always rest assured He understands your every hurt, your weaknesses, even your temptations. Look at what the book of Hebrews says about Jesus Christ, our high priest. "For we do not have a high priest who is unable to sympathize with our weaknesses, but we have one who has been tempted in every way, just as we are—yet was without sin" (Hebrews 4:15). He understands us because, even though He didn't sin, He, like us, was tempted.

Because you were made in His image, you are a child of God and have all the rights and privileges of any other child of God. "Yet to all who received him, to those who believed in his name he gave the right to become children of God" (John 1:12).

You don't have to worry, because God takes care of His children. He loves you and wants only the best for you. For some reason I don't picture God in heaven as a mean ogre of a father who is constantly strict and demanding. I see Him as a loving Father who is actually proud of His children. I think when you try to please Him, He gets a tear in His eye. When I took Christy to her first-grade classroom on the first day of school, I cried. You know what I think? God's eyes were moist, too.

You are His child, and that can't help but improve the way you view yourself. You are not a flop. You are somebody special!

In Christ You Are Forgiven

God makes a big deal out of forgiveness. Often, forgiveness is not our style. It is *always* His style. The concept of forgiveness goes back to the idea that God's ways are different from our ways. *God's forgiveness is forever.* Let me remind you what His Word says: "If we con-

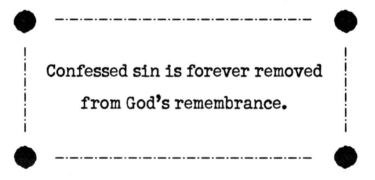

Confessed sin is forever removed from God's remembrance.

fess our sins, he is faithful and just and will forgive us our sins and purify us from all unrighteousness" (1 John 1:9).

Confessed sin is forever removed from God's remembrance. Look how God describes Himself to Israel in the Old Testament: "I, even I, am he who blots out your transgressions, for my own sake, and remembers your sins no more" (Isaiah 43:25). Again we see that God not only chooses to forgive your confessed sins, but He also promises not to remind us of them.

I have a friend who is a psychiatrist. He tells me that we could empty many of the hospital mental wards if people inside them could only understand the freedom of forgiveness. You cannot be free to be all God desires you to be without living as a forgiven person. Because you are a Christian and have confessed your sin to Him, you are forgiven. Your sins are forgotten and that's final.

Because you are forgiven, you are free to be a new creation in Christ. "Therefore, if anyone is in Christ, he is a new creation; the old has gone, the new has come!" (2 Corinthians 5:17).

You may not feel new. At times you may not even act like a new creation. Because of Christ's sacrifice on the cross, however, you are forgiven, you are free, you are new. Go and live like it!

Let me tell you one of my favorite stories—a story that illustrates for me what it means to become a new creation of God. In the musical play *Man of La Mancha*, we meet Don Quixote sitting in a pub in Spain with his faithful servant, Sancho Panza. Don Quixote is a lonely Spanish gentleman who believes he is a knight in the king's service. He isn't really a knight, but no one can tell him differently.

His waitress in the pub is Aldonza, a waitress by day and a harlot by night. Don Quixote takes one look at her and declares, "You shall be my lady. Yes, you are my lady. You will no longer be called Aldonza, you shall be *Dulcinea.*"

She laughs scornfully and shouts, "I'm no lady. I'm only a kitchen slut!"

"No, you are my lady. You are Dulcinea," says the delusional Don Quixote.

You see, every knight needed a lady to inspire him in battle and to whom he would dedicate his victories. Don Quixote believed this harlot Aldonza to be his lady.

Later in the play, some men take advantage of Aldonza. She is raped, the ultimate in indignity. After the men have abused her, she comes back into the pub, her breasts heaving with sobs. She is hysterical. Her blouse and skirt are torn.

Don Quixote cries out, "What is wrong, my lady?"

She can't handle him any longer and screams at the top of her lungs, "Don't call me a lady! I was born in a ditch by a mother who left me there naked and cold and too hungry to cry. I never blamed her. I'm sure she left hoping that I'd have the good sense to die!"

She continues, "Don't call me a lady! I'm only a kitchen slut reeking with sweat. A stranger who men use and forget. Don't call me a lady; I'm only Aldonza. I am nothing at all!" And she rushes into the night, devastated.

Don Quixote calls after her, "But you are my lady, Dulcinea."

In the final scene we see Don Quixote lying in bed, delirious with fever. His faithful servant, Sancho Panza, is by his side. His family, who never believed him to be a knight, are in the room. They are simply waiting for him to die. Don Quixote is moving in and out of consciousness. When it appears that he has completely lost his mind, there is a knock at the door. In walks a Spanish woman in a beautiful, long gown, her head held high, her walk proud and dignified.

She goes to Don Quixote, gets on her knees and puts her hands on his shoulder. She says, "Do you remember me?"

The family tells her he is dying, that he is delirious and has lost his mind. She shakes Don Quixote and says, "You must remember me. I am Dulcinea. You gave me that name."

For a moment, Don Quixote regains his senses and stares at her. He says, "My Dulcinea, I knew you would come." He smiles and then he dies.

Don Quixote had believed the harlot Aldonza to be a Spanish lady named Dulcinea. He believed in her, and she became what he believed her to be.

God believes in you. Because of the forgiving power of Christ, you are a new creation *no matter what you've done or who you are.* God's love transforms you into a new creation.

He believes in you.

He loves you.

You are His child.

You are somebody special!

Part Two

Putting It into Practice

Friends and Self-Esteem

Your choice of friends is a significant factor in determining the kind of person you are and will become. We touched on this in chapter four, but I'm not sure I can emphasize it strongly enough. You become like the people you hang around with.

Friends Have a Profound Influence in Your Life

Since I first got involved with youth ministry in 1971, one of my favorite young people has been a guy named Norman, who wasn't blessed in abundance with beauty, brains *or* bucks. Norman did not have an easy childhood. His dad died when he was in elementary school, and though his mother was great, she worked a lot of extra hours to pay the bills. In no sense could Norman be called handsome. In fact, "Stormin' Norman" looked like the quintessential nerd.

What made Norman unique was that he changed friends and fads about as often as some people change clothes. I met Norman when he was entering eighth grade, and in the few years I was his youth minister, Norman was a:

- Surfer;
- Punk rocker;
- Football team manager;

- Cross-country runner;
- Drummer in a rock band;
- Cowboy (and that's difficult in Newport Beach, California);
- High school band member;
- Drama club member;
- Skateboarder;
- Student body officer;
- Student leader at church;
- Heavy drinker.

Norman moved quickly from one crowd (clique) to another. I never knew what Norman would become next. He was like a chameleon.[1] Every time Norman changed friends he became, in essence, a different person. His new "friends" had a big influence on who he was at that moment. As you can imagine, this influence was not always positive.

Norman had a poor image of himself. One day he confided in me, "I don't really like the *real* Norman, so I'm trying to become someone I can respect. I think if I was accepted by a group of people who liked me, I'd be okay."

Now that was a pretty deep statement for a guy like Norman. In his own way, he was beginning to understand that because he didn't like himself, he was trying to be somebody else. He was also beginning to understand the important truth that whoever you spend time with has a major influence on who you become. We'll come back to Norman later in the chapter.

Choose Your Friends Wisely

Some people never really think about the strong influence friends have on their lives. Because friends do make such a difference in who we become, though, it's extremely important to choose your friends wisely.

Let's take a friendship inventory:

1. Do your friends bring you up or pull you down?
2. What do you like and dislike about your friendships?
3. What can you do to ensure you have quality friends?

When I was a junior in high school, I became a Christian, and I came to realize that the crowd with whom I spent a great deal of time had not been the best influence in my life. One of the best decisions I ever made was choosing a new group of friends that year. It was a difficult decision but, as I look back, it was the *right* decision. When I attended my 10-year high school reunion, it became very clear to

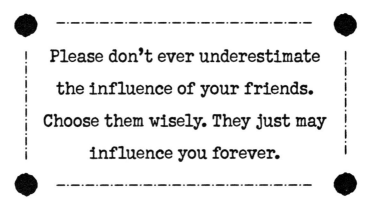

Please don't ever underestimate the influence of your friends. Choose them wisely. They just may influence you forever.

me just how important that decision was in my life. Ten years later my previous friends were struggling with drugs, divorce and failure. My new friends were much more together—and happier.

Sure, this kind of decision is hard. If your need for love and acceptance from others is out of balance because of a low self-image, it will be even tougher. It's also true that the decisions you make today will affect you for the rest of your life. Please don't ever underestimate the influence of your friends. Choose them wisely. They just may influence you forever.

Be Yourself
Sometimes people who have low self-esteem are afraid to be themselves. So they try to be someone else. Donna was dating David. She came to me with a problem. She said, "David thinks I'm somebody who I'm really not."

I told her I didn't understand what she was trying to tell me. She explained, "When I first met David I thought he was really cute and really smart. I knew he was interested in plays, classical music and, you know, the intellectual stuff. Well, I pretended I liked and knew a lot about his world. And he really started to like me."

"Well, what's your problem then?" I asked.

"Now he doesn't know the real me. I know nothing about the

music or literature he's into. But now I'm afraid that if I let him know the real me, he won't like me."

I urged her to take off the mask and be herself. "Donna," I said, "you are a very special person whether you like classical music or not. I imagine David is smart enough to know when he has a good thing, and I wouldn't be surprised if one day he doesn't ask you to marry him. But he must know the real you, and I'm convinced he will love the real you."

One of the great joys of my life was being the minister who married Donna and David a few years later. And you know, Donna still isn't a classical music fan, and David doesn't really care. He loves her for who she is.

Make Positive, Healthy Friendships a Priority in Your Life

Friendship is a priceless gift from God. Few things in life are as important or as wonderful as true friendship. A good friend is a treasure beyond almost anything else in life. Have you made positive,

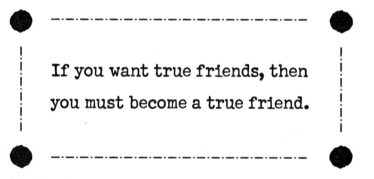

> If you want true friends, then you must become a true friend.

healthy friendships a priority in your life? Think for a moment of three people whom you consider to be true friends. Now take a few moments to list why you consider them true friends. I'm sure there are several reasons you think they're special.

Here's a simple, but important formula. If you want true friends, then you must become a true friend. Let's consider some qualities of a true friend. A true friend is:

1. *Caring and available.* Nothing is more important than the gift of your time and genuine concern.
2. *Encouraging.* When you affirm and support your friends, you are building their self-esteem by *showing* them they are important and that you believe in them.

3. *Willing to sacrifice.* A true friend walks the extra mile and can be depended upon, even when it's inconvenient.
4. *Patient.* No one is perfect, but a true friend will endure even in times of hardship.
5. *A good listener.* Listening is the language of love.
6. *Loyal.* The Bible says, "If you love someone you will be loyal to him no matter what the cost" (1 Corinthians 13:7, TLB).
7. *Truthful.* Telling the truth in love sometimes means telling a friend "the way it is," even if it hurts.

Now, as you look over this list and think about your friends, how do they measure up? How do you measure up? If you need work in one or more of these areas, there's no better time to start than right now.

Christian Friends Will Usually Encourage You to Draw Closer to God

I promised you I would get back to the story of my "nerd" friend, Norman. Sometime later in Norman's high school years, he started getting much more serious about his Christian commitment and the church youth group.

In the church youth fellowship he found a crowd of people who came from different groups at school, but they seemed to get along well at church. He found friends in the church who actually liked him for who he was. They didn't try to turn him into someone else. As Norman became more comfortable with his new Christian friends, he began to open up about his hurts and past mistakes. They accepted him, and he felt loved. He came to understand God's love through the unconditional love of his friends.

It took Norman a long time to believe he belonged. He was building his identity rooted in the love of Christ, though, and the acceptance of positive friendships. His Christian friends *showed* him that God was real, and that reality changed his life. Today, Norman is well on his way to becoming one of the most successful youth ministers in the world.

8

Sex

I want to warn you about this chapter. It's blunt and straightforward. I spent my adolescent years thinking about sex, and I've spent most of my adult years talking to students about sex.[1] I'll be the first to admit that when it comes to sex and self-esteem, I'm opinionated. I didn't start out that way, but after more than 25 years of listening to students ask questions about sex and tell me their stories, I have come to a few important conclusions I want to share with you.

People who have low self-esteem are easily seduced sexually. You show me a person who is sexually promiscuous, and I'll bet he or she is struggling with a poor self-image. Here's a part of a letter I received from a 16-year-old friend in Florida:

> I'm not a bad person. I'm not the best-looking person in the world, but I'm not the worst. I have an okay personality. For the last two years I've had sex with five different boyfriends. I don't know why I always let them have their way, but I do. I guess I want them to like me, and I'm afraid if I don't let them try things (sexually) then they won't want me as a girlfriend.

This is a person who means well, but isn't making wise decisions. Her major problem isn't sex, but low self-esteem. To develop positive and meaningful relationships with guys, she will need to learn to like herself.

When it comes to sexuality, you've probably received some mixed messages. Let me summarize the mixed messages you may be receiving:

- Parents say, *Don't do it*, and then...silence.
- Church tells you, *Don't do it because it's sinful*, and then ...silence.
- School teaches, *This is how you do it*, without discussing morality or values.
- Friends say, *I do it and it's great*, when perhaps they really don't do it so often—and it's not always so great.

Most students don't receive a thorough, positive sex education at home. If you can talk to your parents about sex, you are a fortunate person—and you're in the minority.

Only recently has the Church begun talking about a Christian view of sexuality. Churches are now beginning to realize that, because our culture is so preoccupied with sex, we must discuss this important subject.

Unfortunately, most schools that offer family life or sex education programs provide what I call "value-neutral education." In other words, these programs talk about sex, birth control and technique, but they don't offer any values or moral perspective.

You can often get a bum steer from friends or acquaintances who, because of their own low self-esteem, give you a false impression of the quantity and quality of their sexual experiences.

The result of these mixed messages is confusion.

When I talk to parents about teenage sexuality, I tell them teenagers make sexual decisions based primarily on three factors:

- Peer pressure;
- Emotional involvement that exceeds their maturity level;
- Lack of healthy, positive, Christian sex education.

I know that a person like yourself has some valid questions about sexuality. Let's think through these questions in some practical ways.

Sex

If you have a pulse, you will think about sex. Many people believe they are the only ones who ever think about sex. It's quite natural at your age (or my age for that matter) to have sexual thoughts and questions. I read an interesting statistic a few years ago. Actually, I have no idea whether this is true or not: *The average 16-year-old male has a sexual thought every 20 seconds.*

I shared that quote with a group of students in North Carolina. Afterward, one 16-year-old guy came up to me and said, "You know that quote about a sexual thought every 20 seconds?"

"Yeah," I nodded my head.

"Well, what are we supposed to think about the other 19 seconds?" he asked. "It's always on my mind."

I still don't know if he was serious, but I think you get the point. It's very *common* and *normal* to think about sex.

Sex influences all our lives. Some people think about it more at different ages. Remember that human sexuality is about much more than "doing it" or having a physical relationship. Curiosity about human sexuality begins at an early age. Before they were five years old, each of my three girls were, in their own innocent way, exploring their sexuality. They didn't have crushes on boys then, but were already learning that boys and girls have different plumbing and fixtures.

Along with our God-given sex drive, I can think of at least three reasons sex will be an important factor in your life.

Sex Is Everywhere in Our Culture

One of the main reasons sex influences our lives is that it's *everywhere.* Think of the many rock songs you've heard containing sexual situations, suggestive imagery or even sexually explicit words. Watch one evening of prime-time TV and count all the sexual innuendoes. Even the most innocent movies touch on sex.

Every form of media—newspapers, magazines, radio, television, billboards and now the Internet—at times uses sex to get our attention. Can you think of any advertising slogans that use sex to sell their products? Today, it's hard to think of one that doesn't! The wisdom of the world says that sex sells.

In my neighborhood, a billboard showing a bottle of Tequila, displays the words, "Drink (brand name) Tequila" and a sensual picture of a beautiful woman. She's not wearing anything above her waist. You can see her shapely back, French-cut swimsuit bottom and her face staring seductively at you as you drive by the billboard. I have no idea what the correlation is between a woman's body and Tequila.

I couldn't even begin to tell you what the Tequila bottle looks like, but I can describe that woman's back in detail!

Last year, more than 14,000 acts of sexual intercourse or innuendoes concerning sexual intercourse were aired on prime-time TV alone. Watching soap operas is one of the favorite pastimes of American teenage girls. Did you know that on the "soaps" 94 percent of all acts of intercourse or innuendoes concerning sexual intercourse involve people who are not married to each other? Need I say more? Sex is everywhere in our culture, and it can't help but have an influence in our lives.

Sex Is Mysterious

A few summers ago, Cathy and I went with our friends Steve and Andrea to the beach (without our kids). We were having a wonderful day when, all of a sudden, I started picking up on the conversation of a nearby group of young high school girls talking about their sexual experiences. What can I say? They were sitting right next to us and, yes, I was being nosy. For half an hour I listened to their very loud conversation. Cathy appeared to be sleeping, Andrea was staring out at the ocean and Steve was reading a magazine. For the entire half hour he never turned the page! We were *all* listening. Why? Because no matter what your age, sex is mysterious. We're naturally curious. I've been married for more than 20 years, and I'm still learning about aspects of my sexuality. I think God made sex mysterious because He wanted us to keep it special. When sex quits being a mystery to you, it's time to worry.

Sex Is Enjoyable

Hearing from a Christian minister like me that sex is enjoyable may be a bit confusing. It's the truth, though: Sex can be fun. Now that doesn't mean I believe in premarital sexual intercourse. I firmly believe God wants the best for you, and that's why He makes it clear in the Bible that we are to save sexual intercourse for marriage. Here, however, we are looking at why sex has an influence in our lives, and one of the major reasons is that it's enjoyable much of the time. If it wasn't a very special feeling, it wouldn't be such a big deal.

The reason I tell you sex is fun—and risk possible criticism from your parents—is that I don't want to lie to you. Sex *is* fun. (Of course, I'm not talking here about sexual abuse; "fun" is the last word those who have been subjected to these horrible experiences would use. In general, though, sex is enjoyable).

Statistics tell us that at least 50 percent of all people will have

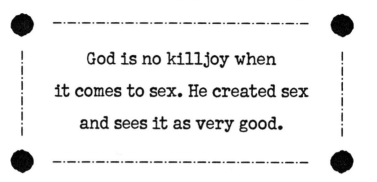

God is no killjoy when
it comes to sex. He created sex
and sees it as very good.

experienced sexual intercourse by the time they are 18 years old.[2] Here are some other important statistics about sex and the American teenager:

- Twelve million teens are sexually active. Eight out of 10 males and seven out of 10 females report having had intercourse while in their teens.[3]
- If present trends continue, 40% of today's 14-year-old girls will be pregnant at least once before age 20.[4]
- Eighty-one percent of today's unmarried males and 67% of today's unmarried females had sexual intercourse before the age of 20.[5]
- Fifty percent of all sexually active 19-year-old males had their first sexual experience between the ages of 11 and 13. Among non-virgins, 50% of the boys and 18% of the girls first had intercourse at age 18 or younger.[6]

It's likely that at least half the people reading this book will have had sex before marriage, even though it goes against God's biblical standards. Some may even have enjoyed the experience, but please, please remember: Just because it can be enjoyable doesn't mean it's right.

What Does the Bible Say?

Recently, a teenage couple sat in my office. They had already been sexually active. She wanted to stop their physical relationship but not break up, and he didn't want to stop anything. At the end of our time together, he looked up at me with a real sense of frustration and said, "Is God the great killjoy when it comes to sex?"

I'm afraid too many people believe that statement to be true when, in fact, it couldn't be further from the truth. Don't forget, sex was God's idea. In Genesis we read that, after God created man and woman—and their sexuality—He looked at what He had made and said that it was "very good." God is no killjoy when it comes to sex. He created sex and sees it as very good.

Some people don't think the Bible has much to say about how we should live out our sexuality. These people haven't done their homework. The Bible is not a sex manual, but it contains several extremely important pieces of wisdom for those who truly desire to be all God wants them to be. Let's take a quick look at a few of the key verses.

The Bible on Adultery

You are probably familiar with the commandment, "You shall not commit adultery" (Exodus 20:14). Adultery occurs when two people have sexual intercourse and at least one of them is married to someone else. You don't need to be an *A* student to realize God knew what He was doing when He included this commandment in His "Big Ten." Most people today have seen lives ruined because of an adulterous affair. I can think of whole families whose lives have been radically changed and deeply hurt because of adultery. God wants the best for you. He wants to protect you from the pain of a broken relationship. He has established this rule for a good reason.

The Bible on Fornication

Paul wrote, "It is God's will that you should be sanctified: that you should avoid sexual immorality" (1 Thessalonians 4:3). Here's a quick Greek lesson! The word translated "immorality" in this verse is *pornea*. It's where we get the root word for pornography or fornication. Some Bible translations even use the word "fornication" instead of "immorality." Fornication occurs when two people who are not married have sexual intercourse.

Again, is God trying to mess up our fun? No way. He knows what's best for us. He loves us. He deeply understands the confusion and heartache caused by those who choose to go against His will. If only you could sit in my office and hear from teenagers their stories of broken relationships. There is guilt, pain, confusion and, for some, a feeling of hopelessness. Again, God surely knew what He was doing when He came up with the command to refrain from sex until marriage.

The Bible on the Union Between Man and Wife

> "Haven't you read," he replied, "that at the beginning the Creator made them male and female, and said, 'For this reason a man will leave his father and mother and be united to his wife, and the two will become one flesh'? So, they are no longer two, but one. Therefore what God has joined together, let man not separate" (Matthew 19:4-6).

God sees a physical, sexual relationship as very sacred and special. The words "casual sex" are not in His vocabulary. There is no more graphic illustration of being united as one flesh than when a man and woman have sexual intercourse. Sexual intercourse is as intimate as you can get. Are you prepared to become one flesh with another person? It's a very serious consideration to make *before* you find yourself in a compromising situation.

The Bible on the Human Body

As a Christian, there is absolutely no doubt that your very own body is a temple of God.

> Flee from sexual immorality. All other sins a man commits are outside his body, but he who sins sexually sins against his own body. Do you not know that your body is a temple of the Holy Spirit, who is in you, whom you have received from God? You are not your own; you were bought at a price. Therefore honor God with your body (1 Corinthians 6:18-20).

I'm not a theologian, but I do know that in a mysterious way God's Holy Spirit lives within each Christian believer. Our bodies should glorify and honor God; after all He lives inside us.

Many verses in Scripture focus on the subject of sex and sexuality other than the ones I've mentioned. It is clear from these, though, that God views our sexuality as very good, very special and even sacred. He's *not* a killjoy! He wants the best for us.

Common Misconceptions About Sex

As I mentioned earlier, the Bible is not a sex manual. God's Word is silent concerning some issues in life. Frankly, I wish the Bible were clearer on the subject of "How far is too far?" I wish it even mentioned the very sensitive subject of masturbation. (Masturbation is the stimulating of one's own sexual organs.) I tackled these issues in another book entitled *Radical Love*, so I'm not going to write extensively here about these same subjects. However, I do want to dispel a few common misconceptions.

Misconception 1: Very few people struggle with masturbation.
Rest assured, this is simply not true. A majority of young people, by the time they reach 18 years of age, will have had a masturbation experience. Curiosity is normal. My strong suggestion is that if you struggle with masturbation, talk to someone you respect about the issue. You are definitely not alone, and there is help and reassurance.

Misconception 2: I will never be tempted sexually.
Because of our human nature and our active sex drive, at one time or another we will *all* be tempted sexually. Conversely, some young people assume that everyone is doing it. Please read and remember the next four words: *Everybody isn't doing it!* A large portion of our teenage population is choosing not to have sex before marriage.

Here's some good advice about overcoming sexual temptation:

Talk about the problem with your girlfriend or boyfriend. If you are going farther than you feel is right and you can't talk about the situation then, frankly, you have a lousy relationship.

Set standards. Some of the best advice Cathy and I ever received before we were married came from our minister. He said, "Set standards *before* you ever reach Inspiration Point." When you set standards and actually talk about it, you know that if you go beyond what you talked about you are violating each other's principles. Far too many people think they can set standards at Inspiration Point. It doesn't work that way!

Plan fun and enjoyable dates in public places. If you honestly don't want a physical relationship, then stay away from Inspiration Point or places that make it easy to yield to temptation.

Let God be a part of your dating life. Pray about your dating relationships. Give God charge over your dating and physical life. When you ask God to take control, it's easier to keep from compromising.

Break up. If you are in over your head sexually—or your partner is pressing you—then the answer is quite clear. Break off the relationship! I understand it's easier said than done, but if you can't work it out, break up. The longer you've been sexually tempted or sexually intimate with a person, the more difficult it is to break up. The sooner the better is the best principle to follow.

Misconception 3:
It's okay to be active sexually, as long as I don't go "all the way."
Too many people are asking the question: "How far can I go? What's the farthest possible I can go physically with my boyfriend or girlfriend and still not offend God?" That's not the right question. It's not how far *can* I go, but rather how far *should* I go? Because the Bible is silent about the specific question of how far is too far, we will have to seek the wisdom of other scriptural principles and the advice of committed Christians.

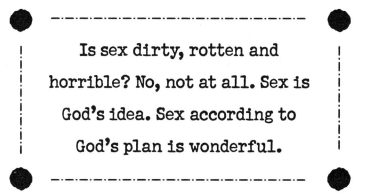

Is sex dirty, rotten and horrible? No, not at all. Sex is God's idea. Sex according to God's plan is wonderful.

The human sex drive is incredibly powerful. Never think you will not be tempted. I think the answer goes back to setting logical, practical, God-honoring standards *before* you find yourself tempted. I've put together a chart that can help you make decisions before you find yourself in trouble. I suggest you take a few minutes and work through this chart. This chart gives you the opportunity to think about your personal philosophy regarding physical involvement with a special friend. Remember to consider these actions in light of the question, What would be pleasing to God?

Before you begin to work on the chart, note that the headings range from *Friendship* to *Marriage*. At the bottom is a list of abbreviations. Each letter stands for a certain action. Write each letter in the column or columns representing the relationship in which you think the action would be pleasing to God. For example, "SI" for "sexual intercourse" has already been placed in the *Marriage* column. We know God's will for intercourse; it is clearly set forth in the Bible. For the other actions listed, thoughtfully, logically and prayerfully determine the standards that will best please and glorify God.

Is sex dirty, rotten and horrible? No, not at all. Sex is God's idea. Sex according to God's plan is wonderful. When you learn to wait—to reserve sex for marriage—you are deepening your positive self-image and pleasing God at the same time.

Setting Standards: God's View

How Far Should I Go?

Friendship	Dating	Steady	Engagement	Marriage
				SI

L = Looking
h = Holding hands
H = Holding hands constantly
HH = Hugging
k = Light kissing

K = Strong kissing
F = French kissing
B = Fondling the breasts
SO = Fondling the sexual organs
SI = Sexual intercourse

Dating

Some of my friends may question how I could have the audacity to write to you about dating. After all, I'm the guy who on his first date spilled an entire plate of spaghetti down the front of his shirt. The plate landed upside down on my lap, and I was wearing white pants. I'm the guy who went to pick up a date in high school on the wrong night, arriving at her door just as she was leaving with her older and bigger boyfriend with whom I thought she had broken up. Even my wonderful wife, Cathy, fell asleep on our first date on the way to dinner. Really!

Well, I may not have had hundreds of dating success stories, but I do know that love and dating were important factors in the development of my self-esteem. I believe that *who* you date and *how* you date say a lot about your Christian commitment and how you feel about yourself.

You may be thinking, *But I don't date yet.* That's a matter of what you consider dating to be. It's true, our culture has turned the great American date into something that's supposed to be romantic and expensive. One 17-year-old friend told me, "My dating life could be summed up with three *M*'s: McDonald's, Movies, Make out."

In actuality, dating happens any time you are relating to the opposite sex. When you drive together to camp in your parents' station wagon with two guys and three girls, in a real sense that's a date. Walking home from school together is a date. Sure, it's not roses and a five-course, candlelight meal, but any time you are with someone of the opposite sex and there is interaction, then I consider that part of the dating process. I'm the last person to be down on romance, but I do think our culture has put way too much pressure on you to have romantic dates when in reality there are lots of other kinds of dates besides the romantic rendezvous.

Some Issues About Dating to Ponder

Forty percent of all high school students graduate without ever having one romantic date.

This may seem hard to believe, but I've read that statistic in many books. Whenever I mention it to adults, we take a poll of their experience; it's about right. Many people think they are the only ones who never date romantically. That's simply not true. I know some very special people who didn't date romantically until they were out of high school, and I know many who now wish *they* hadn't dated so early in life. Their emotional involvement exceeded their maturity level, and they got themselves into trouble sexually.

Caution: Exclusive dating may be hazardous to your love life.

There are two kinds of dating—exclusive and inclusive. Exclusive means it's just the two of you. It's steady and it's serious. Inclusive means you are relating to many friends of the opposite sex. An inclusive date is five girls and four guys who go to the mall together. It's three guys and two girls who meet at someone's home for pizza and a video. Most of us have misunderstood dating. We think it always has to be one on one. It doesn't.

I knew a young couple we nicknamed "the Clingers." Wherever they went they clung to each other. One was almost never seen without the other. When they finally broke up, neither had any good friends because they had invested all their time and energy in each other. Here's some good advice: Even if you do have a steady boyfriend or girlfriend, don't exclude other friendships. The sign of a good relationship is that there is not an overdependence on one another to meet most of your relationship needs.

Dating will be a decisive factor in how you carry out your Christian commitment.

As I stated earlier, you show me who you date and how you date, and I can tell a lot about your Christian commitment. One of the most practical ways to practice your faith is in your dating life.

I'm always asked one major question: "What's your opinion about Christians dating non-Christians?" That's a more important question than many realize. First of all, let's get something straight. Christians and non-Christians have a great deal in common. As we look at the lifestyle of Jesus, we see a God/man who definitely spent time with nonbelievers. I'm convinced we should socialize with non-Christians. However, I'm concerned about Christians dating non-Christians, even on a semiserious level. The Bible is clear that believers should not marry nonbelievers. "Do not be yoked together with unbelievers" (2 Corinthians 6:14). It doesn't say anything about dating, but in a practical sense, dating is practice for marriage.

Does this mean you shouldn't have non-Christian friends? No. Does this mean Christians are any less sexually tempted or promiscuous? Not necessarily. If you are a Christian and Jesus is Master of your life, then there will tend to be a conflict of interest with someone who has a different master for his or her life. Remember, it's just as easy to fall in love with a nonbeliever as with a believer.

Radical Respect: A Christian Approach to Love and Dating

There really is a major difference between the world's philosophy about dating and the Christian approach. The apostle Paul summed up the Christian attitude when he said, "Do nothing out of selfish ambition or vain conceit, but in humility consider others better than yourselves. Each of you should look not only to your own interests, but also to the interests of others. Your attitude should be the same as that of Christ Jesus" (Philippians 2:3-5). Our job is to consider another's interest even above our own.

David and Donna are Christians. They like each other. David is not just dating Donna, a very cute girl who has a beautiful smile and a terrific personality. David is dating Jesus, who lives within Donna. David, too, is a very special person. He is kind, good looking, smart and a great soccer player. But there is more. David has Jesus Christ living inside him by the power of the Holy Spirit. This means Donna is, in a spiritual sense, dating Jesus who lives inside David. The bottom line is, *I am to treat my date as if Jesus lived in him or her.* We are called to radically respect God's children. A major difference between love and sex is this: If you love someone, you want the very best for that person.

Love or Infatuation?

Here's an important fact. The average person falls in love five times between the ages of 13 and 19. You may have a major crush on some

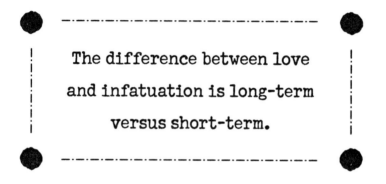

The difference between love and infatuation is long-term versus short-term.

guy or girl. You may even say, "I think I'm in love." Your parents might dismiss it as "puppy love," but puppy love is real to puppies! When I look back at my younger years, I was always falling in love with some girl. (I definitely went over my limit of five). For me it was:

Age 12   Chris
Age 13   Jennie
Age 14   Nancy, then Geri (Geri was a girl!)
Age 15   Marla, back to Jennie
Age 16   Carla and Carol (at the same time!)
Age 17   Carol
Age 18   Carol
Age 19   Cathy (this one lasted!)

Yet, there was a major difference between the love I have for Cathy and the infatuation for, let's say, Nancy. I liked Nancy, but after a few months we mutually decided to go our separate ways. I knew I loved Cathy because there was a *long-term* commitment. We still loved each other even through the hard times.

The difference between love and infatuation is long-term versus short-term. One day, Cathy, our girls and I were enjoying the day at the beach. I was doing my usual people watching. A group of teenagers was mooning over the lifeguard. One girl was loudly proclaiming, "He's such a hunk! I'm in love, I'm in love."

I asked Cathy what she thought of the lifeguard. Even she declared, "He really is very handsome."

When the lifeguard slipped down from his tower and walked to the water the one young girl said, "I want to marry this guy. I've got to meet him."

I laughed at her idea of marriage before meeting him and went back to enjoying the sunshine. However, I wanted to say, "Excuse me, but you're not in love; you're in infatuation."

The lifeguard story may be an exaggeration for you, but far too many people make life-changing decisions in situations almost as silly. Here are some practical guidelines and questions to help you know if you are truly in love:

Do you "like" the other person? There is a difference between "love" and "like." In way too many marriages the people "love" each other, but don't like each other. Those marriages are pretty pathetic. It's possible to love someone without liking him or her, but don't settle for that in a relationship.

Are you transparent with each other? A sign of true love is that you can share your deepest doubts and deepest dreams, disagree on the finer points and still feel accepted.

Are you overly dependent? True love means you want the best for the other person and that you do not have an unhealthy dependence on the other person to meet all your needs.

Is your love (or their love) self-centered? If the question What's in it for me? is often asked in your relationship, then the love is selfish and it's not true love.

Is your love for Jesus as mature as your love for each other? A love that is tied together with the love of God is the strongest kind of love. If you can't answer yes to this question, then I think your relationship is a gamble.

Does your relationship bring you happiness or unhappiness? I know several students right now who are staying in a "love relationship" even though it brings them a great deal of unhappiness. Their low self-esteem is forcing them to hang on. I have a word for these people: *Foolish.*

Love, First Corinthians 13 Style

Here's a great definition of love.

Love:

is patient,

is kind,

is not jealous,

is not conceited,

is not proud,

is not ill-mannered,

is not selfish,

is not irritable,

does not hold grudges,

is not happy with evil,

is happy with the truth.

No one has perfect love but God. However, this can be a great measuring tool for your love relationship. Take a look at the previous list and think of someone you love or who loves you. Now write the words, "seldom," "sometimes" or "almost always" next to the words that describe your love relationship. It's a good exercise to see how the relationship is really going.

Creative Dating

People are far too boring when it comes to dating. Many couples always do the same thing at the same time in the same place. Dating was meant to be fun and enjoyable. For years I've kept a list of creative date ideas in my desk for Cathy and me. People say, "Variety is the spice of life," and we've sure tried a variety of dating experiences. I would say that renting a canoe on a very cold evening at dusk, getting lost and then tipping over the canoe with our clothes on was our dumbest choice for a date. Ten years later, though, it's fun to tell the story. We've created some memories for a lifetime.

Here's what I do. I collect date ideas. I get them from friends or books, and I even brainstorm with students at some of my speaking engagements. You can make your own list, but I'll help you get started. The following are 101 ideas for creative dates:

1. Write a song together.
2. Skip rocks—have a contest.

3. Write a "quickie" letter to a friend.
4. Read the newspaper, *Time* magazine or another informational magazine.
5. Write a letter to God.
6. Call someone to whom you haven't talked in a while and visit with them.
7. Take a walk with your dog.
8. Go to the golf driving range.
9. Watch a Little League baseball, soccer or football game.
10. Write goals.
11. Read a *good* book together.
12. Write a journal.
13. Celebrate anything.
14. Make up a fun diet.
15. Wear a funny hat.
16. Kidnap a friend for breakfast.
17. Take pictures.
18. Go to the park and draw (birds, sunset, etc.).
19. Visit the library and ask the librarian a bizarre question.
20. Develop a new laugh together.
21. Visit the zoo.
22. Visit a mission.
23. Visit an art museum.
24. Ride bikes.
25. Learn a hobby together.
26. Wash a car.
27. Wash your dog.
28. Roller skate.
29. Climb a mountain.
30. Climb a tree.
31. Eat creatively one whole day for $1.18.
32. Picnic anywhere—be creative.
33. Survey the neighborhood with a self-made, bizarre questionnaire.
34. Shop for cars.
35. Go to the airport and watch people.
36. Run your own neighborhood day camp for one day.
37. Go square dancing.
38. Ride a bicycle built for two.

39. Visit a beach or lake.
40. Ice skate.
41. Shop.
42. Play backgammon.
43. Canoe.
44. Go horseback riding.
45. Play pinball or miniature golf.
46. Water ski.
47. Bowl.
48. Try writing a poem or short story.
49. Play ping-pong.
50. Play board games or card games.
51. Plant a garden together.
52. Take a walk.
53. Fly kites.
54. Try hiking.
55. Visit a batting cage.
56. Play tennis.
57. Learn racquetball.
58. Sail.
59. Fish.
60. Ride a ferry.
61. Attend a Bible study.
62. Go for a drive.
63. Snow ski.
64. Jog.
65. Get involved in handicrafts.
66. Take a fun class together.
67. Go on a scavenger hunt.
68. Do homework together.
69. Collect something.
70. Play croquet.
71. Go river rafting or tubing.
72. Play badminton.
73. Build a tree house.
74. Ride motorcycles.
75. Take an exercise class together.
76. Go out to dinner, casual or fancy.
77. Share a pizza and talk.

78. Have a barbecue.
79. Cook dinner for your parents.
80. Take an ice cream break and talk.
81. Cook dinner together.
82. Bake cookies.
83. Make homemade ice cream.
84. Attend a play.
85. Go to the movies.
86. Support school functions.
87 Party with friends.
88. Go to a sports event.
89. Visit a swap meet, an auction or garage sale.
90. Watch TV at someone's house.
91. Go to a concert.
92. Watch hang gliders.
93. Go to a public lecture.
94. Hear a public speaker.
95. Feed the ducks.
96. Go to the circus.
97. Go to the park and swing.
98. Go out in the snow and build snow people.
99. Visit an observatory.
100. Go to the county fair.
101. Find a way to volunteer together.

Getting Along
with Your Parents

When I was a teenager, I had a normal up-and-down relationship with my parents. Mom was a very nice woman. Unquestionably, she has more patience than anyone I have ever known. She raised four Burns boys (and my Dad) and still kept her sanity. Actually, she was pretty bright. I used to try to embarrass her whenever I could get away with it. Whenever an adult male was outside watering his lawn and we were driving by in our car, I would roll down the window, whistle at him and duck down, giving the impression that my mom had whistled. Boy, would she get mad!

Then one day when I was in seventh grade, she cured my whistling forever. I was madly and passionately "in love" with Chris Morris. Chris was the most popular girl in the seventh grade. She was a foot taller than I and, unfortunately, barely knew I existed. My mom and I were on the way to the store when I pulled my usual whistle/duck stunt. This time my mom calmly made a U-turn in the middle of the street, drove directly into Chris Morris's driveway and started honking the horn. It was one of my all-time most embarrassing moments as Chris and her mom looked out the window. My mother calmly asked me if I would ever whistle and duck again. I begged her to drive away and promised never to do it again!

My Dad is a real character. He loves to pull a good practical joke, and he seems to delight in making me the recipient. This next story is about one of his more devastating practical jokes. I can laugh about it now...almost.

On the first day of college, I couldn't keep my eyes off Cathy Boyd. She was stunningly beautiful, and her radiant smile took my breath away. (Am I romantic, or what?) Although I had not yet met her, I vowed to myself that I would ask her out on a date. I remember telling two new friends whom I had met that very day, "See that girl over there?" I pointed at Cathy.

"Yeah, she's cute," they replied.

"Well I'm going to ask her out." They looked at this beautiful girl. Then they looked at me. And they laughed!

To make a long story short—okay, it's not that short, but bear with me, it gets better—Cathy and I became good friends. We weren't boyfriend and girlfriend (her choice, not mine), but I was certain that would happen one day. I told my mom and dad that I thought I had found the girl I would marry. My dad asked if I had taken her out on a date yet, and I said, "No." He laughed, too.

Anyway, the big day came for me to bring her home to meet my parents. Remember, we were not boyfriend and girlfriend. In Cathy's words, we were "just friends." Nevertheless, I asked my mom to fix a special dinner, borrow Aunt Marian's china and create a memorable dining atmosphere. I asked my father to be on his best behavior, begging him not to pull any of his famous practical jokes.

When Cathy and I arrived home for dinner, the table was set. Honestly, it was the nicest our home had ever looked. I don't know if Cathy could tell, but my mom and even my dad were a little nervous. They were both almost overly friendly to Cathy.

We sat down to dinner. My dad was to the left of me, Cathy to the right and my mom across from me. Mom asked me to pray. I closed my eyes and prayed. This was a great moment in my life, to have Cathy at our family dinner table. After I completed my prayer, I took a very large gulp out of the glass of milk in front of me.

My taste buds quickly informed me, however, that this was not regular milk, but buttermilk. *I hate buttermilk.* While we were praying, my Father had switched his buttermilk for my regular milk. I looked out of the corner of my eye and could see him laughing while Cathy and my mom were oblivious to my problem. My mind was racing, and I considered getting up from the table and rushing to the bathroom. The only real choice I had, though, was to be tough...and swallow it. I tried. The buttermilk oozed its way down my throat to my stomach. My stomach flatly would not accept it. My stomach and esophagus had a quick argument, and the next thing I knew, I was spitting up milk all over the tablecloth, food and everybody's plates!

My dad laughed. My mom was furious with my dad. Cathy exclaimed, "How gross!" And I wanted to crawl in a hole and die. That is, I wanted to die only after I had strangled my father. Despite this experience, Cathy eventually married me and, to this day, buttermilk has never been served in our home.

I must be honest with you. I have been very fortunate to have wonderful parents. As I got older, I realized they weren't perfect. I do count my blessings, though, because it wasn't as difficult for me as it is for many who will read this book. Regardless of how you would rate your parents on a scale from 1 to 10, your parents play an important role in the way you see yourself.

I thought parenting was easy until I became one. My life changed dramatically 14 years ago when Christy Meredith Burns entered our home. I had to throw out some of my former ideals and seriously reevaluate this parenting business. Parenting is scary and difficult. To help you get along better with your parents, let me share a few ideas about why I think parents act the way they do.

Nobody Sent Them to Parent Training School

You are probably their first family. Sure, they were raised in a family, but there is a major difference between being a kid in a family and being a dad or mom. I figure by the time I complete all my educational goals, I will have been in school for more than 20 years—mostly to prepare me for my career. In all that time, I didn't take one, single class about parenting kids.

Let me tell you something about me as a father. I experiment on my three girls. I've changed my philosophy about discipline at least a dozen times. Our oldest girl, Christy, was raised differently than Rebecca or Heidi were. We parents learn by trial and error. Just when I thought I had it all figured out with Christy, Rebecca came along.

Her personality and outlook on life were totally different; and Heidi had the gall to be different from either of her sisters.

The first word out of Christy's mouth was "Dada." I expected the same from Rebecca. Not so. Rebecca said "Poopoo" before she said "Dada." When the day finally arrived that Rebecca looked up at me with outstretched arms and said "Dada," I cried. Fifteen minutes later we were out in our front yard and the neighbor's dog went walking by. Rebecca pointed to the dog and again said, "Dada."

I am the first to admit that I'm a work-in-progress as a parent. There are days I am very confident, and then there are other days when I just don't know what I'm doing.

Your Parents Are Running Scared

Your parents may never tell you this directly, but they are running scared when it comes to raising you. They know how easy it is to really blow it. Rest assured that, just like you, they made some pretty silly mistakes when they were your age. I honestly believe most parents mean well, but they tend to overcompensate for their own past failures or family background.

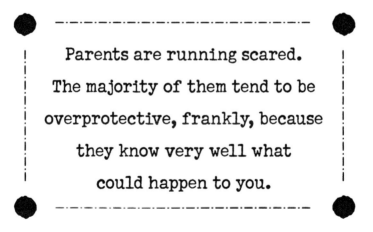

> Parents are running scared.
> The majority of them tend to be
> overprotective, frankly, because
> they know very well what
> could happen to you.

For example, when I was a junior in high school, my dad took me aside and said, "Your mother and I are going on a trip to Florida. Your grandmother will stay with you. I know you are dating Carol pretty seriously, so I'm telling you—while we are gone, don't *do it*. You may get tired, and you've got some very important basketball games coming up while we're gone."

Do you know what my dad was trying to say? He was trying to say, "Jim, I'm concerned about your relationship with Carol. It's normal for young boys and girls to be curious about sex. I'm hoping you will choose to refrain from having sexual intercourse. In fact, I'd like you to consider a number of important issues about saving sexual intercourse for the person you marry. If you ever have any questions, please don't hesitate to ask me. I want to be available to discuss these important issues with you. I love you, and I believe in you."

Because his parents had never talked to him about sex—and he was scared I would do something foolish—he just told me not to do it, gambling that my desire to win a basketball game was greater than my sex drive! If you're wondering what happened during their trip to Florida, Carol broke up with me two days before my parents left. Grandma and I watched a lot of TV.

Parents are running scared. The majority of them tend to be overprotective, frankly, because they know very well what could happen to you. When you think they don't understand, it may well be that they understand all too much.

Parents Are in the Protection Business

Did you know that by the time you are 18 years old you represent an investment of more than $100,000? Never once have I thought of my girls merely as a "financial investment," but I *have* invested my life, energy, time, emotions and finances in my daughters.

Cathy and I will occasionally go out for a romantic dinner away from the kids. We need the break. We decide to dress up and spend some money on a great romantic meal, and we end up spending the evening talking about—you guessed it—"the kids." My parents are in their seventies, and when they go out to dinner *they* still talk about "the kids"!

Parents often express their care and concern in overprotective ways. If you think you can change your parents overnight, forget it. When you were born, they started protecting you. Just because you are now an adolescent, don't think this will immediately change. The best advice I can give you is to be patient and earn their trust.

Your Parents May Be Going Through Their Own Identity Crisis

If you are a normal teen or preteen, you probably have, at one time or another, experienced a typical adolescent identity crisis. After all, that's part of what the teenage years are all about—finding your own identity. Don't think for a moment, though, that this process will magically end with adulthood. Your parents may be having a major attack of identity crisis themselves. I know some parents of teenagers who are panicked by the thought of growing older. I've heard myself say, "What will I do when I grow up?"

"Nobody likes me."

"I don't have any friends."

"I'm scared about the future."

Just yesterday I told Cathy, "I can't believe we are going to this fancy restaurant and I have a big zit on my chin."

We parents aren't much different than you are when it comes to self-esteem and the search for identity. Sometimes we just fake it better.

Building a Good Relationship with Your Parents

Learning a little more about why your parents act the way they do won't always help solve problems immediately. It *will* help you communicate in a more informed manner, though. I hear five common complaints all the time from teenagers about parents. They are: (1) my parents don't trust me; (2) my parents don't love me; (3) my parents don't listen to me; (4) my parents pick on me; and (5) my parents are hypocrites. These complaints may all be true, to a degree. When you were very young, there wasn't a whole lot you could do about your parents' problems. As you move from childhood to adulthood, though, some of the burden of building and maintaining a good relationship must now rest on your shoulders.

Here are four principles to help you get along better with your parents.

Honor and Obey Your Parents

I'm no biblical scholar, but it's pretty clear that the Bible challenges us to honor and obey our parents. Of the Ten Commandments it's the only one with a promise. "Honor your father and your mother, so that you may live long in the land the Lord your God is giving you" (Exodus 20:12).

I don't want to sound overly simple or naive, but I'm convinced that if we make a conscious choice to honor and obey our parents, we will be much happier in the long run. It's a proven fact that people who are happier and not in conflict with loved ones tend to live longer, more successful lives. That verse written thousands of years ago is still true today.

You may be asking, "But what if my parents are absolutely wrong?" My answer is, as long as it is not harmful to God, still honor them. Obey them even if you disagree because that way you will gain their trust. Does it mean you should never have a disagreement? No way. The best of families have their hassles. It does mean you should choose your battles wisely. It isn't worth going to war about every single issue. My suggestion to you is to *consider the long-term results.*

Many people your age want more freedom from their parents. I can certainly understand that. The right way to gain the trust of your parents is to allow your actions to lead the way. If you want their trust, *avoid sneakiness.* As a parent, the way I figure it is this: Where there's smoke there is usually fire. If my girls are being sneaky, then I know they can't be trusted.

I saw a poster the other day showing a picture of a little boy having a guilty look on his face. It appeared he had just been caught doing something wrong. The caption read, "When I'm good, I'm good. When I'm not, I'm human." No one expects you to be perfect. Here's the best thing you can do when you mess up: *Take responsibility for your action.* I tell Christy regularly, "If you tell me the truth, you won't be in trouble. If I catch you telling me a lie, you're in trouble." When in doubt, be honest.

Thank Your Parents

You may not understand this yet, but the odds are great that your parents think they are sacrificing their lives to give you a better one. To some extent, they are probably right. We tend to take for granted the people who give us the most. So if you want a better relationship with your parents, don't forget to express your gratitude. When was the last time you thanked them for all their time, effort, hard work and, yes, even their input in your life?

When I was growing up, we weren't a family who expressed our love in verbal ways. My mom was more comfortable making me a batch of cookies. My dad wouldn't miss one of my baseball games. You couldn't often catch them giving me a hug or telling me they loved me, though.

After I went away to college, I realized how grateful I was to my mom and dad for raising me the way they did and sacrificing so much for me. One weekend I came home determined to thank them and tell them verbally that I loved them. I kept waiting for the right moment, and it never came. As I was leaving, I went over to my dad, put my arms around him and said, "Thanks, Dad, for all you do. I love you."

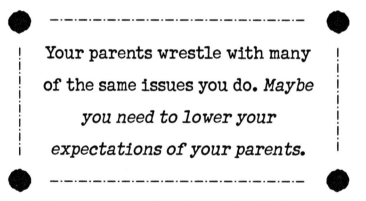

Your parents wrestle with many of the same issues you do. *Maybe you need to lower your expectations of your parents.*

I turned to my mom, gave her a hug and said, "I love you, Mom. Please know how grateful I am for all your hard work."

As I turned to leave, both of them had tears in their eyes. I got in my car and cried halfway back to my college dorm. That was a turning point in our family. We still aren't huggy-kissy, lovey-dovey the way Cathy and I are with our girls, but my parents and I are much freer to express our love and gratitude.

If you haven't told your parents you love and appreciate them, there is no better time than right now to do it!

Try to Walk in Your Parents' Shoes

By this time you may be thinking, *Hey, give me a break. Quit focusing on my parents' needs.* I assure you that when I talk with parents, I am your greatest advocate. Right now, however, I am addressing you, and I'm convinced that one of the most important things you can do to achieve a happy family and a better self-image for yourself is to attempt to understand the struggles your parents are experiencing.

Your parents wrestle with many of the same issues you do. I wouldn't be surprised that if you have low self-esteem, so does your mom or dad. Your home life will be better when you understand where they're coming from.

Sometimes they're burnt out from their work and financial pressures. They say the wrong things and take the wrong actions, just as you and I do at times. Your parents might not express to you all the love you need, but then they probably didn't receive all the love they needed from their parents.

Does this justify their actions? No. Does it help you to understand the family dynamics that are taking place? Yes. *Maybe you need to lower your expectations of your parents.*

When I was a child, I thought my mom and dad were perfect. In my mind, they could do no wrong. Then as I grew older I began to see some of their weaknesses. My first reaction was anger and hurt. My heroes, whom I had put on a pedestal, were falling—hard—off that pedestal. Yet the experience of removing them from the expectation of perfection helped me to take more responsibility for my own happiness and not blame my parents for my emotional state. After all, they were just human—like me.

Are your parents (whether single or married) acting a certain way toward you because of their own relationship struggles? What are the financial pressures on your parents today? Where do you see the major stress areas in their lives? When you walk in their shoes, it doesn't make the problems disappear. It does, however, give you a better understanding of why they act and react the way they do.

Let me ask you three questions to help you apply this principle in your life:

- What problems and pressures are your parents having right now?
- How are these issues affecting their relationship with you?
- What can *you* do to help your parents?

Communication Is a Key
You can never quit working on the communication process. If you

stop working at it, the relationship will deteriorate rapidly. Undoubtedly, one of the other reasons your parents sometimes run scared is that they know how difficult it is to talk to you. Good communication is complicated by the fact that you and your parents are from different generations and have a host of different interests. Perhaps they came from families that didn't communicate very well and now, years later, some crummy habits and patterns have formed.

We can't do very much about the past, but we definitely can make a difference in the future.

Initiate conversation. One of the major complaints of parents is that "my kids don't talk to me." Surprise them. Share your feelings, hurts, joys and dreams. If they don't respond the way you want them to, then later tell them your feelings. If you feel it's a one-way conversation, then persevere. If you must, take the lead when it comes to conversation.

Spend time with your parents. Long after your friends from school have come and gone, you will still have your parents. Most likely you are extremely important to them. As you grow older, they are afraid you don't want to spend time with them anymore. Do something together with Mom and/or Dad in *their* world. If your dad likes baseball, but you aren't particularly fond of it, purchase the tickets and invite him to go with you to a game. He knows you don't love baseball, but he will also know you want to spend time with him—and that's what's important.

Take your mom or dad out on a date. One of the best investments you can make to improve communication with your parents is spending individual time together. Once a month I have a date with each of my girls. We never spend a lot of money on these dates, but I guarantee you it's always one of the high points of my month. I'm always amazed at what we talk about on these dates. I let the girls plan the date and I pay! Don't wait for your parents to ask; they may never get around to it.

God gave you your parents. This is a difficult concept for some people to understand. They *know* their parents aren't perfect. Perhaps a messy divorce, alcoholism, emotional abuse or a hundred other devastating issues has made it difficult for them to believe that God had anything to do with their parent relationship. I know a young woman who was adopted at birth into a pretty negative home. She once told me, "If God had a part in taking my birth parents away from me and giving me these parents, then the joke was a cruel one."

I understand; I really do. However, no one ever promised it would be easy. No one, including God, ever promised you perfect parents. The Bible is clear, though, about God's role in your very creation. David the psalmist put it this way:

> For you created my inmost being; you knit me together in my mother's womb. I praise you because I am fearfully and wonderfully made; your works are wonderful, I know that full well. My frame was not hidden from you when I was made in the secret place. When I was woven together in the depths of the earth, your eyes saw my unformed body. All the days ordained for me were written in your book before one of them came to be (Psalm 139:13-16).

You were placed in your family for a reason. When I first heard this concept as a new Christian in my Campus Life Club in high school, it was as if a light were turned on inside me. It meant that I was somebody special. God had a distinct plan for me. The God of the universe cared enough about me to place me with Bob and Donna Burns in Anaheim, California. Were they absolutely perfect parents? Not really. I haven't been a perfect son either. When I look at them as God's special gift to me, however, I see the relationship in a whole different light.

Here's my last piece of advice about parents. Don't fight it; accept the fact that they will be your parents forever and ever. Because they will be the only parents you have for eternity, do everything you possibly can to keep the relationship growing and positive. It will take time, energy, a lot of work and God's help, but the results will be worth it.

Garbage In/Garbage Out: The Influence of Rock, Movies and TV on Your Self-Esteem

Many years ago, a man was traveling across the country by sneaking from one freight train to the next. One night he climbed into what he thought was a boxcar. He closed the door, which automatically locked shut and trapped him inside. When his eyes adjusted to the light, he realized he was inside a refrigerated boxcar, and he became aware of the intense, freezing cold. He called for help and pounded on the door, but all the noise he made from inside the car failed to attract anyone's attention. After many hours of struggle, he lay down on the floor of the railroad car.

As he tried to fight against the freezing cold, he scratched a message on the floor explaining his unfortunate, imminent death. Late the next day, repairmen from the railroad opened the door and found the dead man inside. Though the man had all the appearance of having frozen to death, the truth was the repairmen had come to fix the broken refrigerator unit in that car. Most likely the temperature of the railroad car had never fallen below fifty degrees during the night. The man died because he *thought* he was freezing to death.

Perhaps nothing is more powerful in the world than the human mind.

Your mind matters, and how you choose to think will have a major influence about nearly everything that happens in your life. The Bible says, "As he [a man] thinks in his heart, so is he" (Proverbs 23:7, *NKJV*).

Ralph Waldo Emerson wrote, "Man becomes what he thinks about all day long."

Many times we forget both the positive and negative influences our minds can have on us. If you ever hope to live out your dreams and choose to live a positive, healthy lifestyle, then one of the major areas of your life you'll want to work on is what you allow to enter your mind.

Your mind is so powerful and yet so vulnerable that whatever you put into it will eventually come out. If you put garbage into your mind, then garbage will come out. If you put good things into your mind, then good things will come out. Life is an echo; you get back what you put into it. If you tend to plant negative thoughts, then what do you suppose will grow inside your mind?

Powerful Influences

Pornography

I recently conducted research in the area of pornography and its effects on teenagers. Do you realize that more than 10 billion dollars are spent on pornography in America each year? When you fill your mind with garbage, then the natural tendency is to take it a step farther and act upon what you've ingested. Half of all American teenagers have at least some exposure to pornography once a month. No wonder so many people have such trouble in the area of their sexuality.

If you are tempted to expose your mind to pornography, even if you think it's innocent, don't do it. I've met people who are addicted to pornography. It started out innocently, but they developed a hunger for more and more. Today they are very confused people experiencing deep hurts in their lives. Absolutely nothing is positive about pornography. I wish they would print billboards that read: *Caution: Pornography Is Poison to Your Mind.*

Television

I'm not going to tell you to burn your TV set; but perhaps it's time to think about what comes into your home and into your mind through television. Your TV set is not inherently sinful, but it isn't neutral either. For example, the average high school student attends school approximately 1,000 hours a year. The same student watches more than 1,200 hours of TV during the same year. The average person watches 15,000 commercials a year—and 15,000 of anything is bound to have an effect on you. Have you ever thought about what TV commercials are telling you? TV commercials teach us, subtly, that:

1. All problems are resolvable.
2. All problems are resolvable quickly.
3. All problems are resolvable through the aid of some technology.

Actually, your mind takes an active part in this deception in the way it processes these powerful images. You may come to believe that if you buy a certain pair of jeans or drink the same brand of soft drink Michael Jackson drinks, then you will find happiness.

The beer commercials are some of the cleverest on TV. Sometimes, I enjoy the commercials more than the program they're sponsoring. Why is it, however, that most alcohol commercials show beautiful,

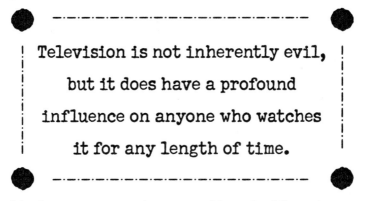

Television is not inherently evil, but it does have a profound influence on anyone who watches it for any length of time.

healthy, happy young people enjoying life to the fullest when more than 3 million teenage alcoholics are addicted to a life that is anything but happy?

Life may be falling apart all around us, but our minds subconsciously tell us everything will be all right soon. After all, it always turns out okay on our favorite television programs. If we aren't careful, TV soon becomes our reality. The power of the subconscious mind and the influence of television are so powerful that we can forget it's make-believe. A few years ago, more than 250,000 people wrote to Dr. Marcus Welby, M.D. requesting serious medical advice. Dr. Welby was not a real doctor, but a TV character! Were all these people crazy? No, they were normal people like you and me who just forgot that TV is a fake. If you are a couch potato or a "teleholic" addicted to TV, don't think your problem is innocent. Television is not inherently evil, but it does have a profound influence on anyone who watches it for any length of time.

Rock Music

Today's teenagers are unified by one common interest more than any other: rock music. The latest surveys tell us that the average student listens to four hours of rock music a day, and more than 85 percent of all American young people claim rock is their favorite kind of music.

Given these kinds of statistics, we must conclude that rock music plays a significant role in your life. Even when you do not realize it, your mind is recording *everything* that is placed inside it, even on a subconscious level.

In the Christian world, the subject of rock music is very controversial. Some people who have good intentions believe all rock music is literally satanic. Others, who have just as strong convictions, say it's okay to listen to the majority of rock music. However, you'll never hear anyone from a Christian perspective say that what some call "pornographic rock" is a positive influence for our lives.

People frequently ask me where I stand in the rock-and-roll debate. I am personally somewhere in between the two extremes. I am deeply concerned about the subtle—and not so subtle—lyrics coming out of the mouths of rock superstars. I know our minds pick up on the lyrics even when we aren't focusing on the words to the songs. The power of the mind is awesome and not to be taken lightly. I have seen hundreds of people lose ground in their relationship with God because, frankly, their choice of music didn't leave room for their Christian faith. One of the Old Testament writers said, "Choose for yourselves this day whom you will serve" (Joshua 24:15.) I think lots of teenagers, when asked that question, would lean closer to rock-and-roll than to the Rock of our salvation.

On the other hand, just because a song is played on a rock station or has a more progressive beat, I don't necessarily label it *evil*. I'm much more concerned with the words than with the beat. I've heard some very raunchy lyrics from some of my parents' slow country-and-western songs. Basically, you have three options:

1. I won't listen to rock music at all.
2. I will constantly listen to rock music.
3. I want to be a selective listener.

Although many teenagers choose option 2, I hope you won't. Studies of the subconscious mind lead me to believe it's just too dangerous to your lifestyle. Most teens say they don't listen to the lyrics, but when they are asked the words of the songs, even they are surprised at how much of a song they can repeat from memory.

Here are some excellent questions and guidelines for listening to rock music (or any other kind of music):

· Can I glorify Christ by listening to this song?
· Am I using my time wisely?
· What has control over me?

When you are being totally honest and seeking God's wisdom, these simple questions will help you make the right choices. They will help you intelligently choose what kind of music you will and will not invite into your mind.

Winning the Battle for Your Mind

Media can fool you. Never underestimate the incredible power of music, movies, TV, videos, magazines, cyberspace; the direct influence they have on your mind is frightening. The Garbage In/Garbage Out principle is the strongest and most sensible principle for dealing with the media. If you feed your mind with negative influences, the negative *will* come out. If you feed it with positive messages, then the positive will win. It's really quite simple. What goes in must come out. Because your mind is so much a part of who you are and who you are becoming, let's look at a few practical suggestions for improving your thought life.

Think About Good Things

Here is a sentence for you to memorize: *I create change in my life when I gain control of my thoughts*. People who live fulfilled lives are in the process of mastering their thought life. Listen to the apostle Paul's sound advice about your thought life:

> Whatever is true, whatever is noble, whatever is right, whatever is pure, whatever is lovely, whatever is admirable —if anything is excellent or praiseworthy—think about such things. Whatever you have learned or received or heard from me, or seen in me—put it into practice. And the God of peace will be with you (Philippians 4:8,9).

Notice what Paul said is the result of thinking about good things—*peace*. When you plant good thoughts in your life, the roots will grow

> **Prepare yourself to think good thoughts: read and memorize Scripture, choose friends who will build you up, listen to good music and read inspiring books.**

deep. When the seed of good thoughts begins to sprout, one of its many positive characteristics is peace.

Program Your Mind to Think Good Thoughts

Let me suggest a few ways to prepare yourself to think good thoughts: read and memorize Scripture, choose friends who will build you up, listen to good music and read inspiring books. In your time of prayer, don't rush it. Take your time praying and thinking. Remember, "As a man thinks in his heart, so is he."

Developing a quality devotional life has always been a struggle for me, yet I believe it is paramount to thinking good thoughts and keeping my focus on the Lord. In frustration a few years ago, I developed a plan that worked for me. I wanted to read through the entire New Testament, so I divided it into 90 sections, approximately three chapters a day. On my appointment calendar, I placed a big mark 90 days from the day I began. Reading the New Testament completely through in a three-month period helped me discipline myself to read for 10 to 15 minutes a day, and it gave me the opportunity to plant good things in my life.[1]

If you truly want to program your mind for good thoughts, then you will want to find a devotional method that works for you. In my studies of the great men and women of God, I learned that they shared one characteristic that stands out above all others: They all had a daily quiet time with God.

If you want to think good thoughts, you must "renew" your mind constantly with good input. Two Scripture verses have been especially helpful to me:

> Thou dost keep him in perfect peace, whose mind is stayed on thee, because he trusts in thee (Isaiah 26:3, *RSV*).

> Do not let this Book of the Law depart from your mouth; meditate on it day and night, so that you may be careful to do everything written in it. Then you will be prosperous and successful (Joshua 1:8).

God promises that if we focus our minds on Him we will have peace, prosperity and success. The work required to discipline and focus your mind on God will be worth it.

The apostle Paul challenges you in this, saying, "Do not conform any longer to the pattern of this world, *but be transformed by the renewing of your mind*. Then you will be able to test and approve what God's will is—his good, pleasing and perfect will" (Romans 12:2, italics mine).

That is really what we are after—a renewed mind. When you have a renewed mind, you can dare to dream. God works through minds that are renewed, refreshed and open to His Spirit. Take a moment to relax and clean out your mind. Then put down on a piece of paper a few thoughts about your innermost dreams and righteous desires. Don't be afraid to let your imagination run wild. Now put the words *I can do all things through Christ who strengthens me* (Philippians 4:13, *NKJV*) on that piece of paper. With a renewed mind, what is holding you back from becoming the person of your dreams?

Don't Dwell on Things over Which You Have No Control

Too many people are consumed with worrying about things they cannot control. Don't forget, 85 percent of what we worry about will never happen, 10 percent will happen anyway and only 5 percent are justifiable worries. Talk about wasted energy! *Worry paralyzes your ability to live productively.*

Have you ever done something really stupid? Something you regretted doing? Of course you have! Is there anything you can do about it now? If your answer is yes, then do it today. If your answer is no, then *quit worrying about it* and use your energy on something productive.

I like Paul's attitude toward life. "Forgetting what is behind and straining toward what is ahead, I press on toward the goal to win the prize for which God has called me heavenward in Christ Jesus" (Philippians 3:13,14).

Paul's attitude is highly therapeutic for those of us who tend to get stuck on our past failures. Give your past to God and look toward a bright and beautiful future!

Our bodies—emotionally, spiritually and physically—were not meant to handle as much pressure and as many worries as we tend to take upon ourselves. Again, Paul offers good advice:

> Do not be anxious about anything, but in everything, by prayer and petition, with thanksgiving, present your requests to God. And the peace of God, which transcends all understanding, will guard your hearts and your minds in Christ Jesus (Philippians 4:6,7).

Paul clearly states that we are not to worry about anything, but that we are to hand our problems over to God. Again, notice the result—*peace.*

I have a friend who is always worried and hassled with one "major problem" or another. She tends to compound her worries by playing the *What if?* game. She looks for the worst in life and is constantly asking, "Well, what if there is a tragedy?" or "What if he doesn't like me?" or "What if I can't do it?" My reply is that we have enough problems each and every day. The *What if?* worry game only clouds the picture and keeps us from enjoying the here and now. If you play the *What If?* game, decide now to quit playing. It's a game you can't win.

Your Words Have Power

"Death and life are in the power of the tongue" (Proverbs 18:21, *NKJV*). What you say aloud often comes back to haunt you. In fact, what you say often reveals what you are thinking—and sometimes it comes out when you wish it hadn't.

If you constantly give yourself "verbal beatings," putting yourself down, it will only be a matter of time until you live as if those verbal beatings were true. The self-fulfilling prophecy says, When you call yourself dumb, you will become dumb. When you call yourself ugly, you will become ugly. If you say that you have no friends, you will eventually become friendless. Words have power.

Cheryl Pruitt won the Miss America title in 1980. When she was four years old, she lived in a little town in the South. Every day the milkman would deliver milk to her father's general store. He would pick up little Cheryl in his arms and say, "How's my little Miss America?" As she got older, he would wave to her on the street and shout, "How's my little Miss America?" Cheryl said that by the time she was 10 years old, because of the milkman's words, she was very comfortable with the idea of being Miss America. And that's exactly who she became. Your self-talk is a key to who you will become. Never underestimate the power of what you say to yourself.

The Power of the Mind Is a Terrible Thing to Waste

Your mind is your most powerful possession. Use it or lose it. Learn to use the power of your mind to add positive insight to your life. During the Vietnamese conflict, many servicemen spent years in the horrible conditions of prison camps in North Vietnam. It was amazing how many of our heroes came out with very sharp minds and spirits. Many of the prisoners of war have shared how they used the power of the mind to better themselves, even in the most horrible of situations.

Many of these men learned foreign languages from each other, while others actually memorized entire books from the Bible without ever having a Bible in prison. Perhaps the greatest illustration of the power of the mind I've ever heard comes from Colonel George Hall, who was a "guest" of the North Vietnamese government at the notorious, hellish prison camp known as the Hanoi Hilton. Every day he practiced golfing in his mind. He daydreamed playing the greatest courses in the world, always using the proper positioning, correct backswing and perfect follow through. While a POW he practiced literally thousands of times.

Only one week after his release, Colonel Hall entered the New Orleans Open. This man, who had never been anything but a duffer, shot a 76—what professionals who practice daily often shoot. What an amazing score for someone who had not touched a real golf club for seven years—especially someone who had been living in a prison camp!

There is power in your mind. Don't waste it. Your mind matters. You can choose how you think.

Making Wise Decisions About Drugs and Alcohol

Jimmy G. never did anything halfway. His energy, enthusiasm and zest for living were contagious. Jimmy pursued God, life, bikes, sports and even girls with 100 percent, almost reckless abandon.

Cathy and I met Jimmy months after he had moved from Philadelphia to California when he was in the eighth grade. His mom, twin sister and he had packed all their belongings in the middle of the night and fled an abusive, alcoholic father. Jimmy seldom talked about him, but I knew it hurt him never to see his father. In a real sense for Jimmy, I took the place of his father.

We watched Jimmy grow up. He started to do better in school. Jimmy took care of the two precious women in his life by getting a job at age 16. He never missed a church youth group meeting and somehow always talked me into scholarship money for every camp or retreat our church sponsored. We had some great times together.

Then things began to change. Jimmy started to experiment with beer and alcohol. He really wasn't any different than his other friends, but his reaction was different. Jimmy could drink a six-pack of beer and it wouldn't phase him. He was always the designated driver. He became known as the guy who could handle his alcohol. As he began to drink more and more, there were times he would go overboard and get drunk. But usually he could drink twice as much as anyone else with little or no effect...or so we thought. By this time

I had moved away, but I began hearing negative stories about Jimmy. The passion he had for other positive aspects of life was consumed by drinking and, later, drugs. Then he simply disappeared.

Years later Jimmy showed up on our doorstep. He was a heavy cocaine user and a dealer. His story was typical for an addict: broken relationships, problems with the law, family fights and straying from God. As I looked at this young man who had been so full of life, I started to cry. He was now so empty. To see me so upset shook him, but it really didn't help in the long run. That meeting with Jimmy took place several years ago. Today, I have no idea where Jimmy is or even if he is still alive. He's probably in jail.

I need to be honest with you. Back then I didn't know how to help Jimmy. He was a good kid with great potential and faith in God who, when he started experimenting with alcohol, really didn't know what hit him. Today, after years of study, with an awareness of alcoholism in my own family background and after watching hundreds of students like Jimmy come and go, I could offer some very positive, healthy solutions. Perhaps something in this chapter will help you to make the right choice about using alcohol or drugs.

The Power of Drugs and Alcohol

Jimmy was not a bad person. He was not stupid or rebellious. Jimmy was a great person with outstanding potential who never understood the devastating power of alcohol and drugs. Because Jimmy's father was an alcoholic, it is very likely that Jimmy had a natural *predisposition* toward alcoholism and drug addiction. If you come from a family where there is alcoholism or drug addiction, the odds are high that you could develop the same problem.

Alcoholism and drug addiction don't just happen to weak individuals who have low self-esteem. That's a myth. Alcoholism and drug addiction can enslave anyone, regardless of age, intelligence or religious faith. The bottom line is that if you have a history of alcoholism and drug addiction in your family, don't even gamble with experimentation.

Second, Jimmy had a *high tolerance* for alcohol. He was the guy who could drink all night and it didn't seem to phase him as it did others. When people were praising him for his ability to "hold his liquor," they should have been warning him that those who have a high tolerance level for alcohol can easily become addicted. The people who, after one glass of wine, fall asleep or get sick usually don't become problem drinkers. What Jimmy didn't know is that his body was different. It *craved* alcohol, and his high tolerance only postponed his eventual problems.

If you've experimented with drinking or drug use, and it didn't affect you much, then you should seriously consider never drinking or taking

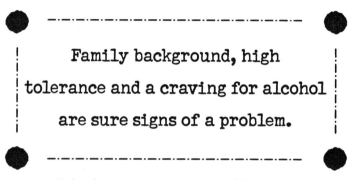

Family background, high tolerance and a craving for alcohol are sure signs of a problem.

drugs again. High tolerance is a warning signal. It may mean you have a body that can easily become addicted to alcohol and drugs.

Family background, high tolerance and a craving for alcohol are sure signs of a problem. If I could have helped Jimmy recognize those symptoms early in his experimental phase, perhaps he would never have fallen victim to addiction.

In recent years, I have spoken to thousands of students about drugs and alcohol. People are polite; they listen, laugh a little at my jokes, ask a question or two. I'm afraid, though, the vast majority walk away thinking, *It will never happen to me.* The truth is, even if you come from a relatively stable Christian background, earn above average grades and possess a very positive self-image, you are not immune to problems with alcohol and drugs.

Here are the facts. By the time you graduate from high school, the chances are:

- 88 percent of your class will have experimented with alcohol;
- 57 percent of your class will have tried an illicit drug;
- 33 percent of your class will smoke marijuana on occasion;
- 33 percent of your class will get drunk at least once a month;

- 25 percent of your class will smoke marijuana regularly;
- One in six of you will have tried cocaine or crack.

You cannot assume it will never happen to you. It's necessary to make proper decisions at an early age about drugs and drinking—and then stick to your convictions. You are dealing with something much more powerful and destructive than the experts initially thought. My friend Steve Arterburn, a national authority in the field of drug and alcohol addiction, tells students, "What you see is *not* what you get."

On television, hundreds of beer commercials with clever slogans feature athletic young men and women enjoying some form of friendly competition. Today, more than 15 million people are alcoholics in America alone, and most of them started young consuming an innocent drink of beer.

The people in liquor ads look so together. So why is the suicide rate 58 times higher among alcoholics than for the general population? More than 50 percent of all automobile fatalities are caused by someone driving under the influence.

Surely not one of the thousands of families who lost a loved one in a traffic accident last year agree with the beer slogan that says, "It doesn't get any better than this." What you see is not what you get.

Why Students Take Drugs and Drink Alcohol

When I was in seventh grade, I was invited to *the* party of the year with *the* popular group. In my mind I'd made it. I was *in*. While at the party, I kept noticing people sneaking out to the yard. The next time a group slipped away from the party, I followed them out front. Andrew Peers picked up a bottle of tequila from out of the bushes and passed it around. When they handed me the bottle I didn't know what to do. I didn't want to drink, but I wanted to be accepted by that group. My desire to belong quickly became stronger than my desire not to drink. I took a long, hard "swig" of the tequila. I hated the taste, and the rest of the night I felt crummy. When I got home, I threw up.

If I didn't like the taste, and I really didn't want to drink, they why did I go ahead and do it? That's easy. *Peer pressure.* I so badly wanted to belong, I would have done almost anything to be accepted. My perception of that evening was, *If I don't drink they won't like me.* So I compromised my convictions to be a part of the crowd. Would they not have accepted me as a part of the group if I had never ventured out into the yard? As I look back on the experience, I doubt if it really mattered. From the perspective of a seventh grader who had fairly low self-esteem, however, I sure thought it did.

Most students start drinking, smoking or taking drugs because of peer pressure or out of curiosity. Unfortunately, many get hooked before they fully understand what's happening to them. They don't recognize the other factors compounding their potential problems. Some of those other factors are:

- *Biological predisposition.* Those who have a family history of substance abuse have what is universally agreed to be a genetic, or hereditary predisposition to chemical dependency.
- *Parental attitudes.* If your parents drink or take drugs regularly, there is a far greater chance you will follow in their footsteps. I have one word for you: *Don't!*
- *Life crisis.* During periods of stress, many teens turn to the bottle just as adults do. It's a false manager of stress.
- *Depression.* When students get depressed, many attempt to mask their depressed feelings with a quick fix of alcohol or drugs. It works for a short time, but the depression doesn't go away. In fact, it will get worse.

Why do students use alcohol and drugs? It all boils down to this; teenagers use alcohol and drugs because:

1. It makes them feel good and
2. It works every single time.

No one disagrees that the teenage years bring extra stress and sometimes pain. Some students find that putting a foreign substance in their body will make them feel better...for a while. They come to depend on drugs and alcohol to take away the pain; but relief is only temporary. When the high is gone, their problems resurface.

What Happens When Teenagers Use Drugs and Alcohol?

What substance users don't realize is that something else very important takes place when they use drugs and alcohol to replace their pain. *They stop learning how to cope with stress.* Drug and alcohol use is a false coping mechanism for dealing with stress. It makes

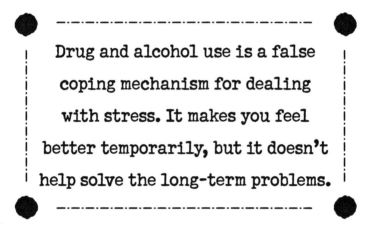

Drug and alcohol use is a false coping mechanism for dealing with stress. It makes you feel better temporarily, but it doesn't help solve the long-term problems.

you feel better temporarily, but it doesn't help solve the long-term problems. You wake up the next morning with the same problems, sometimes intensified, and you're forced to decide again how to cope with the stress.

Substance abuse happens in stages. No one becomes an alcoholic after one party. However, as a student stops learning how to cope, usage will escalate until he or she is in the throes of addiction. Consider the stages leading to chemical addiction:

1. *Experimental phase.* The occasional use of drugs or alcohol.
2. *Social phase.* Regular usage at parties in increasing amounts.
3. *Daily preoccupation.* Perhaps the use of harder drugs and the beginning signs of dependency appear.
4. *Chemical addiction.* A preoccupation with getting high. In this stage there is a loss of control, and people will violate their value system.

I appreciate the slogan that has appeared on walls in many schools in this country: *Drug Abuse Is Life Abuse.* For many, the story of drug use starts off innocently, but the ending is never happy.

Gateway Drugs

Before you make a decision about using alcohol and drugs, it's important to have *all* the facts. The media have tended to focus their coverage on the latest, most exotic drugs. Their reports concern drug smugglers in foreign lands and the hot new drug gaining popularity on the street. Meanwhile, thousands of teenagers are becoming physically and mentally addicted to the more common "gateway drugs." These are the drugs that, all too often, prove to be a "gateway" leading to the stronger stuff.

The path to drug addiction is well-documented, having claimed millions of victims. Most of these individuals followed these steps:

1. Beer or wine;
2. Hard liquor and/or cigarettes;
3. Marijuana;
4. Cocaine, heroin and other illicit drugs.

Generally, no one moves to step 4 without first going through steps 1, 2 and 3. Consider these interesting facts about the gateway drugs.[1]

Tobacco
Eighty-five percent of those who experiment with cigarettes will become addicted to nicotine—some after smoking as few as five cigarettes! Cigars, a trendy choice among teen smokers since 1995, contain up to 40 times the nicotine found in cigarettes.[2] Smokeless tobacco, or chewing tobacco, is also highly addictive.

Eighty-one percent of young smokers will experiment with marijuana, whereas only 21 percent of nonsmokers will try "grass." According to former White House drug chief Dr. Robert L. Dupont Jr., cigarette smokers between the ages of 12 and 17 are:

- Twice as likely to use alcohol;
- Nine times as likely to ingest depressants and stimulants;
- Ten times as likely to smoke marijuana;
- Fourteen times as likely to use cocaine, hallucinogens or heroin.

Smoking kills more than 52,000 Americans each year through chronic lung disease. Another 4,000 American lives are taken in smoking-related fires, and upward of $30 billion are spent on health-care problems related to smoking each year. Just because it is legal to smoke tobacco doesn't mean it's an intelligent choice. I like what they're now teaching kids in kindergarten: "Be smart, don't start."

Alcohol

Alcohol is a dangerous drug. Though our society mistakenly tends to view it as different from other drugs, alcohol *is* a drug. Alcohol is a depressant, and it causes more deaths among young people than any other drug. Because it's legal and accepted by the general population, many people are unaware that it attacks the nervous system and, over a period of time, can shorten a life. Some parents are actually relieved to discover their kids are "only" drinking and not smoking pot or swallowing pills.

Approximately 15 million Americans are addicted to alcohol, according to the Drug Enforcement Administration and the National Institute of Alcohol Abuse and Alcoholism. The same organizations estimate there are an additional 4.6 million problem drinkers in the United States. More than 100,000 people die each year from the effects of alcohol. An alcoholic has a life expectancy 10 to 12 years shorter than a nondrinker. Up to 83 percent of all fire-related deaths are considered to be alcohol related, and 50 percent of all home accidents are caused by problem drinkers. Alcohol is a factor in 70 percent of all drownings and 40 percent of all industrial accidents. More than 15,000 adult suicides and 3,000 teenage suicides are committed each year by alcoholics. The National Institute on Drug Abuse (NIDA) estimates that 4 million American teenagers are problem drinkers.

Marijuana

Smoking marijuana will usually lead to heavier drug use. Sixty-seven percent of marijuana users move on to other drugs, while 98 percent of those teens who do *not* smoke pot also do not take other drugs. Those of us in junior and senior high school in the 1960s heard Timothy Leary and other drug heroes tell us marijuana was not harmful. They said it was less dangerous than alcohol and caused no hangover. Our generation generally believed this to be true, and at the time no substantial studies had been funded to put our assumptions to the test.

All that has changed, however. For one thing, today's marijuana is up to 20 times stronger than the plants harvested only a decade ago. Furthermore, it has been substantiated that not only does pot contain more cancer-causing agents than tobacco, but it also destroys brain cells and reduces short-term memory retention.

Continued use of this drug can lead to what is called "amotivational syndrome," the symptoms of which include lethargy, reduced attention span, varying degrees of personality change and a general lack of interest in anything but getting high.

Marijuana also diminishes the body's ability to protect itself from illness by reducing the division of disease-repelling white blood cells. Therefore, a person who smokes marijuana regularly is likely to get sick more often than is normal. Marijuana is not the harmless drug it was thought to be in the psychedelic '60s, but a treacherous gateway to heavier drug use.

Making a Decision

Basically, you have three choices concerning drug and alcohol usage:

1. Drink and take drugs as much as you want.
2. Drink and take drugs in moderation.
3. Choose not to drink or do drugs.

If you believe you can drink and do drugs as much as you want, then you are heading for trouble. It's only a matter of time before you face bigger problems than you've ever imagined. The good news for you is that when you crash—and you will—help is available. The bad news is that the pain of addiction may continue for years, and you will share the suffering with those who know and love you. I suggest you visit an Alcoholics Anonymous meeting or a drug and alcohol treatment center and listen very carefully to the stories of the people there. You may one day *be* one of those stories if you continue to live by the philosophy of "do your own thing."

Let me give you something more to think about before you choose to drink or use drugs in moderation. All drug usage is illegal, and drinking under the minimum age is against the law. Christians who wish to drink in moderation must do so within the confines of the law and in accordance with Scripture.

The Bible makes it very clear that drunkenness is a sin.

> The acts of the sinful nature are obvious: sexual immoral-
> ity, impurity and debauchery; idolatry and witchcraft;
> hatred, discord, jealousy, fits of rage, selfish ambition,
> dissensions, factions and envy; *drunkenness*, orgies and
> the like. I warn you, as I did before, that those who live
> like this will not inherit the kingdom of God (Galatians
> 5:19-21, italics mine).

> Do not get drunk on wine, which leads to debauchery.
> Instead, be filled with the Spirit (Ephesians 5:18).

It is impossible to be drunk and under the influence of the Spirit
of God at the same time.

Finally, if you do drink, even in moderation, do not drive. Driving
and drinking don't mix. People who drive under the influence of
alcohol are selfish, foolish individuals who are gambling with their
lives and the lives of innocent people.

If you are from a family that has alcoholism or drug addiction
problems, then I ask you to seriously reconsider your choice to drink
or take drugs in moderation. The odds are too great that you will
develop a drinking or drug problem. If you already have a drinking
problem, then drinking in moderation is definitely not a healthy
option. Quit.

Why I Choose Not to
Drink or Take Drugs

Is it sinful for someone of legal age to have a glass of wine or beer?
Nowhere do I read in the Bible that it is wrong to drink alcohol,
though it's very clear that drunkenness is against God's will.

I've chosen not to drink or take drugs. I don't drink, because I
don't want to render my witness ineffective. If a friend or family
member were to see me drinking a harmless glass of wine, they may
use this singular event to justify their own abusive drinking habit.
They may say, "Well, Jim drinks, so it must be okay."

For me, alcohol is not an option, because I have made a commitment to God not to drink. It is a spiritual discipline. I don't believe every adult must necessarily follow my example, but I do think that with the onslaught of new information about the effects of drugs and alcohol, more people will need to make the same decision I did.

My hope is that you will choose not to drink or take drugs. The age-old adage is true. Play with matches and you are going to get burned. If you choose not to drink or take drugs, you will avoid all the potential dangers of drug and alcohol abuse. I'm sure that's what my special friend, Jimmy G., would tell you...if I could find him.

13

Sexual Abuse

I wish you could have been with me at lunch today. I sat with one of the most outstanding men in our community. He's rich, incredibly handsome and is one of the funniest people I've ever known. I have to be honest with you, at times I play the comparison game with him, and I always lose.

Today was different. He told me of his childhood. Tears were flowing from his eyes as he shared one of the worst sexual abuse stories I have ever heard. He has always looked so together, but, on the inside, this man was falling apart in every way—all because he had been a victim of one of the cruelest crimes imaginable.

His grandfather, whom he loved and trusted, had sexually molested him year after year from age 11 to age 16. My friend had never told anyone, including his wife. He had buried his hurt and pain, but now, as he was coming to grips with his past, he realized his abuse was causing him agonizing torture.

This is a very serious chapter in the book. There is nothing funny about sexual abuse. Nobody really likes to broach the subject. Nobody likes to talk about it, and nobody really wants to hear about it. Yet the cold, hard, frightening facts tell us that sexual abuse affects the lives of millions of people who just wish it would go away.

One out of three young women will be sexually abused by the age of 18.

One out of five young men will be sexually abused by age 13.

These statistics are conservative compared to some of the latest findings that say the problem could be far more widespread.

Sexual Abuse Is Real, and It's Everywhere

If you have been a victim of sexual abuse, these may be the first words about the subject you have read. Yet every facet of your life is clouded by the fact that something very horrible has happened to you. If you have never been sexually abused, the odds are good that someone close to you knows the trauma of sexual abuse only too well.

From my counseling experience, I knew that sexual abuse was a problem. I had no idea, though, just how prevalent the trauma was until I started speaking about the subject. Wherever I go, when the subject is broached, people who are unquestionably devastated by their experience come to me and want to talk.

Let me introduce you to some very special people who were in my youth group. They looked and acted like everyone else, but inside they were keeping a terrible secret that was tearing them apart. All the names and some of the situations have been changed for obvious reasons of confidentiality, but these stories are real.

Bonnie was baby-sitting at her ex-boyfriend Tom's house. She was very close to his little sister and his family, even though Tom and she had quit dating. Tom's stepfather had always been very nice to Bonnie. In fact, she often wished she had a father as special as Tom's stepfather.

Tom's family was going out to dinner and to a play while Bonnie watched the youngest child. The stepfather, Ted, would be home, but he would be working in the back room.

The moment Bonnie put the little girl to bed, Ted came into the kitchen and asked Bonnie if she wanted some popcorn. Bonnie loved popcorn. She said, "Thanks. That will go good with the program I'm watching on television."

Ted made the popcorn, then sat down on the couch next to Bonnie and started watching the program with her. Bonnie complained about a sore back she had gotten from playing softball. So Tom's stepfather began to massage her back. At first he rubbed outside her sweater, but after a while he moved his hands under her sweater.

Bonnie froze. She didn't know what to do. She didn't know if this nice man was going to go farther or was just doing her an innocent favor. Bonnie was tense and nervous. In a soft voice, Tom's stepfather told her to relax; it would be better for her backache. Eventually, Ted began caressing her breasts.

The phone rang. Bonnie was grateful for the distraction. Tom's stepfather, reluctantly it seemed, got up to answer the phone. Bonnie had been sexually abused.

When Monica was nine years old, her older brother molested her. It was a terrible, traumatic experience, which she revealed to no one because her 14-year-old brother threatened to kill her if she told. The next month, her brother raped her. For the next two and a half years, he had sexual relations with her, always vowing to kill her if she told anyone.

Monica never told a soul. Her brother was a violent person and she feared for her life. She withdrew. She flunked most of her classes and experimented with drugs given to her by her brother. Finally her brother was arrested for armed robbery, and Monica was free of the horror of further traumatic experiences.

An acquaintance of Monica invited her to a weekend retreat at a Christian camp. There, for the first time in her life, she heard about God's unconditional love for her through Jesus Christ. She wanted to become a Christian, but her past experiences haunted her and kept her from coming to Christ. After coming home from camp, she made an appointment with a youth pastor and told her story. Monica had been sexually abused.

Steve was seven when a baby-sitter molested him.

Janice, at age nine, heard her parents fighting terribly one night. That evening, for the first time, her father slipped into her room and had sexual intercourse with her. This pattern continued for the next seven years.

Tom's favorite uncle molested him on a camping trip and confused Tom by telling him all uncles "do this" with their favorite nephews.

Older boys in the neighborhood sexually abused Carol. When she told her parents, her mother didn't believe her. Carol's father laughed.

All these people had been sexually abused.

The stories go on and on. Just in the past few months, I have heard horror stories of a brother-in-law videotaping a girl in the shower, older males exposing themselves to innocent children, a date rape, adults sharing pornographic photos and other stories I can't put into writing. It's real and it's everywhere.

Good News for Victims of Abuse

Unfortunately, most people who have been sexually abused in one way or another keep their pain and experiences to themselves. They try to forget about it or simply wish it would go away. Well, it doesn't go away—*ever.* I would go as far as to say that without help, a person who has been sexually abused can never have a healthy self-image or a life free of his or her past.

However, there is good news for those who struggle in this area. Thousands of people who have been sexually abused and sought assistance have been helped. If you are a victim of sexual abuse—or

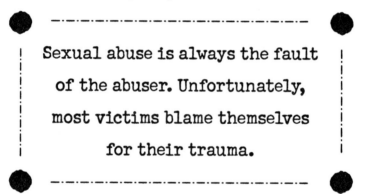

Sexual abuse is always the fault of the abuser. Unfortunately, most victims blame themselves for their trauma.

any other form of abuse—you are not alone. People all around you suffer with the same issues. They are probably dealing with their hurt in a similar way.

Here are four points anyone who has been sexually abused must hear:

1. It's not your fault.
2. Seek help. Don't suffer in silence.
3. There is hope.
4. God cares. He really does.

It's Not Your Fault

Sexual abuse is always the fault of the abuser. Unfortunately, most victims blame themselves for their trauma. It's time to put the blame in the proper place. If someone robbed you and stole your money, or if you were innocently hit by a drunk driver, would you blame yourself?

When you have been sexually abused in any way, you have become a victim of a horrible crime. The abuser is sick. If you blame yourself, then you will get sick, too. *It's not your fault.*

Seek Help; Don't Suffer in Silence

The first step toward recovery is to seek help. Sometimes it's embarrassing. Other times you don't want to reveal a deep, dark family secret. The truth is, though, you will not get better if you don't seek help. If you choose to suffer in silence, you are choosing to get worse, not better. You can't wish away your hurt. You are not the only one who has experienced this trauma. You *can* receive help from a qualified adult counselor.

Jill confided in her youth pastor that, six months prior, she had been at a party where an older guy forced her to have sexual intercourse with him. Jill said she felt "cheap and used," but was afraid to tell anyone. She was even more afraid that, if she did tell someone, it would get back to the guy who abused her.

Her youth pastor did what the law required him to do and reported the rape. As the story unfolded, it was revealed that at least 15 other girls had also been desecrated by this one young man. Jill received excellent support from a counselor who helped her. She dealt properly with the important issues that result from being violated. Jill's progress has been remarkably rapid. Had she waited longer to seek help, she may well have developed destructive behavior patterns that would have taken years to undo. Victims need to seek help to prevent themselves from forever living in a state of turmoil. Please don't suffer alone.

I urge people who have been sexually abused not to wait another day, but to seek help immediately. If you have been sexually abused and have never sought help, then you are reading this chapter for a reason. I believe God wants you to seek help. Talk with someone. It only gets more difficult. It doesn't get easier.

There Is Hope!

If you have been hurt and hurt deeply, then it may be difficult for you to see that life will ever be different. You can draw hope from the knowledge that thousands before you have been set free from the pain after they sought help.

When Sandy was 14, her stepfather abused her in every way. Sandy told no one and acted as if nothing had happened. Her school work did not suffer; it even improved. No one knew her inner pain, until one day she took a bottle of her mother's prescription sleeping pills. When Sandy came to, she was in the hospital. She prayed she would die.

A good psychiatrist asked her if she would be willing to talk about why it hurt so bad that she wanted to die. He asked her if there was anyone she would talk to. She said, "Jim Burns, my youth minister." Sandy and I spent the next several hours together as her story unfolded. She told me that she hated all guys. In her mind, her father had deserted her when she was eight years old. And now this stepfather, who had been a nice man, was sexually assaulting her. The pain went so deep that Sandy had lost all concept of hope.

Together we sought help. We reported this tragedy first to the psychiatrist and then to a social worker who spoke to the mother and stepfather. Sandy went through extensive Christian counseling, which helped her put her life together. Eventually she could see that she had been the victim of a very sick man. The counseling process gave her a reason to live—and a hope that life could be different.

Today she isn't blaming herself. She still feels a tinge of pain when she thinks about the experience, but she has learned to move on. Not only does Sandy have two lovely children, but she and her husband also run a camp for battered and abused kids. She hung on to hope, and I'm sure she would tell you it was the right thing to do.

God Cares; He Really Does

Most people who have experienced any kind of sexual abuse struggle in their relationship with God. Under the circumstances, I can understand the difficulty they have comprehending the unconditional, sacrificial love of God in Jesus Christ. Too many people, however, spend their energy blaming God instead of allowing themselves to be comforted by Him. God wants to walk with you through this valley of hurt and disappointment.

The New Testament tells us how Jesus heard about the death of His friend Lazarus. When He saw the family grieving, "Jesus wept" (John 11:35). Jesus weeps for you, too, when you have been hurt.

Jesus knows a great deal about suffering. After all, He suffered an excruciating, humiliating death on the cross, just to make it possible for you and me to spend an eternity with God in heaven. I believe that Jesus Christ would have suffered on the cross if you were the only person in the world who needed Him.

If God loves you enough to allow His only Son to die for you, then I believe He cares deeply for you and your pain. I've seen the tragic, broken lives of young men and women restored and made whole because they allowed God to reconstruct their past and fill their future with hope. You need to understand that, although it seems

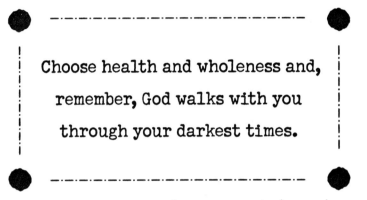

Choose health and wholeness and, remember, God walks with you through your darkest times.

your circumstances may never change, your attitude *can* change—and that makes all the difference in the world.

I love the thoughts written by Margaret Rose Powers. The passage is simply entitled "Footprints."

> One night a man had a dream. He dreamed he was walking along the beach with the Lord. Across the sky flashed scenes from his life. For each scene, he noticed two sets of footprints in the sand; one belonged to him and the other to the Lord.
>
> When the last scene of his life flashed before him, he looked back at the footprints in the sand. He noticed that many times along the path of his life there was only one set of footprints. He also noticed that this happened at the very lowest and saddest times in his life.
>
> This really bothered him, and he questioned the Lord about it. "Lord, You said that once I decided to follow You, You'd walk with me all the way. But I have noticed that during the most troublesome times in my life, there is only one set of footprints. I don't understand why when I needed You most You would leave me."

The Lord replied, "My precious, precious child. I love you and would never leave you. During your times of trial and suffering, when you see only one set of footprints, it was then that I carried you."

If you have experienced sexual abuse in your life, then the battle is now in your hands. The choices are yours. You *can* overcome your pain. The decision to pursue wholeness is not always easy, but it is always the best.

The question I leave with you is this: Who and where do you want to be in 10 years?

The decisions you make today will affect you the rest of your life. Choose health and wholeness and, remember, God walks with you through your darkest times.

What Is Sexual Abuse?

The following information about sexual abuse is something I distribute when I'm speaking to students about this important but horrible subject:[1]

Nobody has the right to touch your body without your permission, regardless of how much he loves you, how much money he has spent on you, or for any other reason.

Any time a touch makes you feel uncomfortable, you have the right to say no. You never *owe* another person the right to touch you. Trust your gut feelings. Pushing, manipulating, pressuring, exploiting or abusing another person is never acceptable in any relationship.

If someone touches you in a way you don't like, tell that person to stop and get away, and then talk about it with an adult you trust.

If an adult or older teenager has touched you in the past, it is *not your fault*. It is *always* the adult's responsibility.

It is *very important* that you get counseling for sexual abuse *now*, to prevent problems as you grow older. If you have never talked with a counselor, seek help immediately.

The sexual assault of a person occurs when a male or female is tricked, coerced, seduced, intimidated, manipulated into cooperating or forced into not offering resistance to sexual activity with another person.

Sexual abuse can be defined as:

- Showing children pornographic materials;
- Taking nude pictures;
- An adult exposing himself to a child or asking the child to expose himself/herself;
- Fondling private areas of the body;
- Intimate kissing;
- Genital contact;
- Intercourse;
- Rape.

Sexual assault includes incest, molestation, rape and "date rape."

Incest is sexual activity between any relatives. Usually this activity is initiated by a father or stepfather, grandfather, uncle, cousin or brother. Occasionally, it will be initiated by a mother, grandmother or aunt.

Molestation is sexual activity with someone outside the person's family. Eighty percent of molestations are by someone the victim knows and trusts: a family friend, the mother's boyfriend, a neighbor, a teacher, a coach, a doctor or dentist, a pastor or priest, a youth leader, a camp counselor or a baby-sitter. Only 20 percent of molestations are perpetrated by strangers.

Rape is forced penetration (by penis or any object) of the vagina, mouth or anus against the will of the victim.

Acquaintance rape or *"date rape"* is rape by someone you know or are dating. Date rapists generally use just enough force to gain compliance. A man may use his physical power to coerce intercourse or take advantage of a situation by using force, pressure, deception, trickery or teen vulnerability. The date rapist is not a weird, easily identifiable person. He is just like anyone else—except that he uses force to get his way.

About 75 percent of teen rapes are acquaintance or "date rapes."

What to Do If You Are Raped

If you are raped:

1. Get to a safe place;
2. *Do not* bathe, douche or change clothes;
3. Call a rape crisis hot line;
4. Go to the hospital emergency room.

Have a friend or family member go with you to the hospital and take a change of clothes if possible. Do this as soon as possible in order to:

- Preserve the evidence (very important if you decide to prosecute);
- Determine the extent and nature of physical injury and receive treatment;
- Test for venereal disease and pregnancy.

Reasons for Reporting the Rape

Reporting the crime to police is a decision that only you can make. However, making a police report will benefit you directly. Reporting the assault is a way of regaining your sense of personal power and control, as it enables you to do something concrete about the crime committed against you. Reporting the crime also helps ensure that you receive the most immediate and comprehensive assistance available.

Making a police report will help prevent other people from being raped. Reporting and prosecuting the assailant are essential to prevent rape. Most rapists are repeat offenders. If the rape is not reported, the assailant cannot be apprehended.

Afterword

A little more than nine years ago, our daughter Heidi Michelle was born with a major heart complication. Within the first week of her life, she underwent two very serious operations. After her first operation, five-day-old Heidi was placed on a Lear jet air ambulance and flown 3,000 miles to Boston, Massachusetts, for the second emergency operation. Needless to say, life for her mother and me was very, very difficult.

During those trying days we experienced pain, worry, exhaustion and doubt, and yet, at the same time, we were overwhelmed with love and support from our church, family and friends. We received hundreds of cards and expressions of love. Of all the messages of comfort and support we received, the words I remember most came from a good friend of mine just weeks after we flew with Heidi back from Boston to our home in Dana Point, California.

When my friend Toby and I met for lunch, he stuck out his hand, looked me in the eye and said, "Burnsie, nobody said it was gonna be easy." Throughout lunch, Toby's words were ringing in my ears. *Nobody said it was gonna be easy.* Not only was Toby right about our situation, but Toby was also right about life. Far too many of us believe that life should be free from pain and struggles; but life is not always fair. No one, including God, promises us a life without difficulty.

Most Christians tend to have the *IT* syndrome: "As soon as I get *IT*, then I will be happy." We make the mistake of thinking the grass is always greener on the other side of the fence. Unfortunately, there is no magical, mystical answer to surviving adolescence. Tough times come to everyone's life. This book is more about *how* you deal with the tough times when they come. When you're prepared for the difficult times, it makes all the difference in how you survive them.

Live Your Life on Purpose

Today, God has given each of us 24 hours to live life to the fullest. That's 1,440 minutes or 86,400 seconds. Maybe it's time to take 30 of those seconds to tell someone you love him or her. Or take five minutes and write a kind note to a friend. How about 20 minutes a day to talk with God? You can tackle most any problem one day at a time. You can accomplish great things one day at a time.

I met Elaine when I was in graduate school in Princeton, New Jersey, in 1975. Life was hard for her. She was confined to a wheelchair and very poor. She never had a boyfriend. Frankly, she was very homely. The cerebral palsy she lived with daily had distorted her face and her voice.

Elaine Robertson is the most radiant woman I have ever met, though. I've never met a person who loved Jesus and other people with such passion.

A few years ago, I ran into her while on a speaking trip in New Jersey. I took her out to lunch at her favorite diner in Princeton along with some of my friends. On the way back from lunch, I wheeled this wonderful woman through the great Princeton University campus. As I pushed her in her wheelchair, I leaned over and said, "Elaine, life's been tough for you, hasn't it? How do you make it so beautifully?"

She said, "Jim, stop the wheelchair. I want to sing you and your friends a song." In her not-so-beautiful voice she sang these words:

Jesus, I love You,
I give You my heart.
I live for You daily,
each day a new start.

She sang those simple words again and again. I looked up at my friends through the tears in my eyes and saw that everyone was thinking the same thought: *That's the answer. It's so simple in this complicated world that we often miss it.*

Live your life on purpose. Life's too short, way too short, to settle for mediocrity.

Notes

Chapter 1: Learning to Like Yourself

1. The idea for this diagram is taken from a similar one in an excellent workbook by Bill Jones, *Self-Image: How to Like Yourself* (San Bernardino, Calif.: Here's Life Publishers, Inc., 1988), p. 19.

Chapter 2: Go for It: Making Good Decisions

1. *The Student Bible* (Grand Rapids: Zondervan, 1986), p. 967.

Chapter 3: Developing a Positive Self-Image

1. James Dobson, *Preparing for Adolescence* (Ventura, Calif.: Regal Books, 1989), p. 21.
2. Ibid.
3. Children who grow up being subjected to put-downs, negative nicknames and constant criticism often become critical adults who have less-than-adequate self-esteem.
4. Bill Bright, *Revolution Now!* (Arrowhead Springs: Campus Crusade for Christ, 1969), pp. 44–45.
5. Tim Hansel, *Holy Sweat* (Dallas: Word Publishing, 1987), p. 136.
6. Jim Burns, *Putting God First* (Eugene, Oreg.: Harvest House Publishers, 1982).

Chapter 4: Peer Pressure and Self-Esteem

1. Boxers are a form of underwear. Other names for them include skivvies, undershorts, drawers, union suit, jockey shorts and unmentionables.

Chapter 6: Good News for Imperfect People

1. David A. Seamands, *Healing for Damaged Emotions* (Wheaton, Ill.: Victor Books, 1981), p. 22.

Chapter 7: Friends and Self-Esteem

1. A chameleon is a slimy lizard that changes hues to whatever color it happens to be next to at the moment.

Chapter 8: Sex

1. Jim Burns, *Radical Love: Finding God's Best for Your Love Life* (Ventura, Calif.: Regal Books, 1995). For a comprehensive look at the subject of love, sex and dating, you may want to read this book.
2. Josh McDowell, *Why Wait?* (San Bernardino, Calif.: Here's Life Publishers, 1987).
3. *Teenage Pregnancy: The Problem That Hasn't Gone Away* (New York: Alan Guttmacher Institute, 1981), p. 7.
4. Robert Coles and Jeffrey Stokes, *Sex and the American Teenager* (New York: Harper Colophon Books, n.d.) (Table 18), p. 73.
5. *Time* magazine (December 9, 1985).
6. McDowell, *Why Wait?*

Chapter 11: Garbage In/Garbage Out

1. Jim Burns, *Growth Unlimited* (Eugene, Oreg.: Harvest House Publishers, 1987).

Chapter 12: Making Wise Decisions About Drugs and Alcohol

1. Stephen Arterburn and Jim Burns, *Drugproof Your Kids* (Ventura, Calif.: Regal Books, 1995).
2. Report by the Centers for Disease Control and *Prevention* magazine (May 22, 1997).

Chapter 13: Sexual Abuse

1. Jim Burns, *The Youth Builder* (Eugene, Oreg.: Harvest House Publishers, 1988), pp. 276–279.

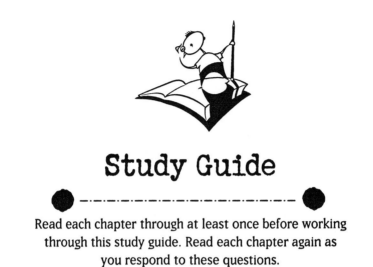

Study Guide

Read each chapter through at least once before working through this study guide. Read each chapter again as you respond to these questions.

Chapter 1
Learning to Like Yourself

The Big Idea:
Your response to what God has already done for you will make the difference between a positive, healthy self-image and a negative self-image.

Discussion Starters:
1. Why do you suppose people have difficulty liking themselves?
2. What are three areas of your life that affect your self-image, either positively or negatively?
3. Jesus said, "Seek first his kingdom and his righteousness, and all these things will be given to you as well" (Matthew 6:33). What do you think He meant by this statement?
4. How will putting God first in your life help you to develop a better self-image?
5. If you could do anything with your life, what great dreams would you dream knowing you could not fail?

Special Experience:
Write out on a piece of paper 25 reasons why you should like yourself. Even though it's often easier to list the negatives in life, this experience can be a powerful reminder of God's goodness in your life.

Related Scripture:
Psalm 25:4-11
Matthew 6:25-34
Philippians 1:6
Philippians 4:13

Chapter 2
Go for It: Making Good Decisions

The Big Idea:
The decisions you make today will play an important part in who you become in the future.

Discussion Starters:

1. List three decisions you could make today that would contribute positively to your happiness in the future.
2. In what areas of your life do you sometimes have difficulty making good decisions?
3. Jesus said, "You will know the truth, and the truth will set you free" (John 8:32). How does this statement of Jesus relate to you personally?
4. Which one of the illustrations in this chapter—Laconia, healing at the pool of Bethesda, Abraham Lincoln, Eagle/Prairie Chicken—can you relate to and why?
5. Who do you know who has a "go for it" attitude? What can you learn from them?

Special Experience:
Interview an adult you really respect. Ask that person what decisions made when your age helped him or her to reach the highest potential.

Related Scripture:
Proverbs 3:5,6
Matthew 7:13,14
Romans 12:1,2
Colossians 3:1-4

Chapter 3
Developing a Positive Self-Image

The Big Idea:

A poor self-image will negatively affect your relationships—with God, with others and with yourself. Developing a positive self-image will strengthen all areas of your life and your faith in God.

Discussion Starters:

1. Which of the three areas of life mentioned in this chapter do you struggle with most, beauty, brains or bucks?

2. What kinds of pressure do you feel from our society that hinder your ability to develop a positive self-image?

3. "For we are God's workmanship, created in Christ Jesus to do good works, which God prepared in advance for us to do" (Ephesians 2:10). How does this verse relate to developing a positive self-image?

4. What are four goals you can set to help you produce a healthier self-image?

5. Read the poem "I Am" at the end of this chapter. What is the message of hope found in this poem?

Special Experience:

God's values are different from those of the world. On a separate piece of paper, make a list of God's values. Then make a list of the world's values. How do each of these values affect your self-image?

Related Scripture:

Psalm 139:13-18
Matthew 22:34-40
Romans 5:8
1 Thessalonians 5:11

Chapter 4
Peer Pressure and Self-Esteem

The Big Idea:

Peer pressure is an extremely powerful influence in our lives. In God's eyes you are special, and with His help you can win the battle against peer pressure.

Discussion Starters:

1. Why does peer pressure have such a strong influence on you and your friends?
2. Why is it difficult to say no when challenged to do something we really don't want to do in the first place?
3. Read Romans 7:15-25. Can you identify with Paul? In what areas of your life do you experience your toughest battles?
4. How can you dare to be different without being weird?
5. Do your friends influence you in a mostly positive or negative way?

Special Experience:

Make a list of all the areas in your life where you currently feel pressured by peers, or where you feel you may be susceptible to peer pressure. Now with the help of a family member, youth pastor or Christian friend, find a Scripture reference to help you resist each temptation.

Related Scripture:

Matthew 7:24-27
1 Corinthians 10:13
James 1:2-8
James 4:7,8

Chapter 5

Handling Your Emotions: Am I Normal?

The Big Idea:

You can prepare yourself for the emotional storms of life that come to everyone.

Discussion Starters:

1. What emotions do you struggle with most in life?
2. Do you agree or disagree with the statement "Life is difficult"? Why or why not?
3. Read Matthew 7:24-27. What can you do to build a better foundation for those times when storms come to your life?
4. Look back at the five principles listed in this chapter to keep your life from crumbling under pressure. Which of these principles are most important in your life right now?
5. What specific action steps can you take this week to handle your emotions better?

Special Experience:

Worry Wart Evaluation: Pick the five things on this list that you worry about the most. Rank them in order and spend time in prayer turning these things over to God.

job	athletics	grades
car	sister/brother	parents
relationship with God	club activities	clothes
dating	sex	friends
homework	looking good for others	

1. What can you do to reduce these worries?
2. Why do you think we worry even when we don't want to?
3. Do you tend to blow your worries out of proportion?

Related Scripture:

Psalm 23	Hebrews 13:5
Philippians 4:6,7	1 Peter 5:7

Chapter 6
Good News for Imperfect People

The Big Idea:
Even with all your flaws, God believes in you, loves you and calls you His child. You are somebody special in God's eyes.

Discussion Starters:
1. What makes it difficult for you to accept God's forgiveness in your life?
2. When you think of the unconditional love of God, what stories from the Bible help remind you of this love?
3. "But God demonstrates his own love for us in this: While we were still sinners, Christ died for us" (Romans 5:8). How is this verse good news for those who aren't perfect?
4. How can the sacrificial love and forgiveness of God help your self-image?
5. What do you think it means to be a "new creation in Christ"?

Special Experience:
Write down as many of your own mistakes and sins as you can think of on a piece of paper. Ask God to forgive your sins and then burn the paper. The burned paper is symbolic of God's forgiveness, which is forever.

Related Scripture:
Isaiah 1:18
John 3:16
Hebrews 10:17
1 John 1:9

Chapter 7
Friends and Self-Esteem

The Big Idea:
Your choice of friends will be a significant factor in determining the kind of person you are and will become.

Discussion Starters:
1. Do you agree or disagree with this statement: You become like the people you hang around with?
2. Answer the "Friendship Inventory" questions found on page 64 of this chapter.
3. The special friendship of David and Jonathan is one of the most inspiring stories in the Old Testament. How does 1 Samuel 20:14-17 demonstrate the qualities of encouragement and loyalty in this friendship?
4. True friendship is costly. What do you think it takes to develop a strong friendship?
5. Name a situation where you had to make a personal sacrifice to keep a struggling friendship going.

Special Experience:
Write an affirming note to a special friend telling the person why you appreciate his or her friendship. You may also want to write a note to one of your parents affirming your friendship with them.

Related Scripture:
Proverbs 17:17
John 15:13-15
1 Corinthians 13:4-7
James 4:4

Chapter 8
Sex

The Big Idea:

Sex is an important issue in the lives of young people, and God deeply cares about your sexuality.

Discussion Starters:

1. Is sexual promiscuity on your school campus as prevalent as most parents think it is?
2. Why do you suppose television, rock music and movies all deal so much with sex?
3. The Bible says, "Do you not know that your body is a temple of the Holy Spirit, who is in you, whom you have received from God?" (1 Corinthians 6:19). How does this verse relate to your sexuality?
4. What do you think it means to let God be a part of your dating life?
5. What steps can you take now to prevent you from being a sexually active teenager?

Special Experience:

1. Look through the latest copy of almost any magazine you can purchase at a store and try to find as many sexually oriented advertisements as you can.
2. Take two minutes and write down as many popular songs as you can remember that have a sexual theme.

Related Scripture:

Proverbs 7:6-27
Matthew 5:27,28
1 Corinthians 10:13
2 Corinthians 6:14

Chapter 9
Dating

The Big Idea:
Dating will be a decisive factor in how you carry out your Christian commitment.

Discussion Starters:
1. Do you think there is too much pressure to participate in romantic dating at your school?
2. How would you summarize the difference between love and infatuation?
3. The Bible says, "Do not be yoked together with unbelievers" (2 Corinthians 6:14). What's your opinion of Christians dating non-Christians?
4. How can dating affect your self-image?
5. Describe the kind of person you would like to date.

Special Experience:
Make your own list of creative dates, or take the best ones from this chapter and have a creative date party. Invite both guys and girls to your house and enjoy some of the most creative dates you can think of.

Related Scripture:
Matthew 5:8
Romans 12:9,10
1 Thessalonians 4:3-8
2 Timothy 2:22

Chapter 10
Getting Along with Your Parents

The Big Idea:
God gave you your parents, and now you must take some of the responsibility to make the relationship work.

Discussion Starters:
1. How has your opinion of your parents changed over the years?
2. What qualities do you appreciate most in your parents? Tell them!
3. One of the Ten Commandments is, "Honor your father and mother, so that you may live long in the land the Lord your God is giving you" (Exodus 20:12). What does this verse actually mean?
4. What would you say are your greatest struggles with your parents right now?
5. What action steps can you take to enjoy a better relationship with your parents?

Special Experience:
Plan a special date, trip or event for you and your parent(s) to experience together. Without telling them what you are going to do, work out the details, including paying for the experience. You may be shocked at their positive reactions.

Related Scripture:
Psalm 139:13-16
Proverbs 6:20-22
Matthew 5:9
Colossians 3:20

Chapter 11
Garbage In/Garbage Out

The Big Idea:
Whatever you put into your mind will eventually come out!

Discussion Starters:

1. Do you agree or disagree with this statement: Life is an echo; you get back what you put into it? Why?
2. What is your philosophy about listening to rock music? Watching television and movies? Pornography?
3. What do you think Paul meant when he wrote, "Whatever is true, whatever is noble, whatever is right, whatever is pure, whatever is lovely, whatever is admirable—if anything is excellent or praiseworthy—think about such things" (Philippians 4:8)?
4. What are the best ways for you to "renew your mind" (see Romans 12:2)?
5. What practical steps can you take immediately to improve your thought life?

Special Experience:
Have a contest among your family members or youth group to see who can find the most negative influence from a night of prime-time television programming or in any popular magazine.

Related Scripture:
Proverbs 23:7
Matthew 12:34
Philippians 4:6,7
Colossians 3:1,2

Chapter 12
Making Wise Decisions
About Drugs and Alcohol

The Big Idea:
Your decision about the use of drugs and alcohol will be one of the most important decisions of your life. You should be aware of the short-term and long-term effects and ramifications of using drugs and alcohol.

Discussion Starters:
1. Do you think the national average of drug and alcohol use quoted in this chapter are similar to the statistics at your school?
2. Why do you think kids drink alcohol and do drugs when it is illegal?
3. The Bible says, "Do not get drunk on wine, which leads to debauchery. Instead, be filled with the Spirit" (Ephesians 5:18). What is the importance of this verse?
4. List several ways you could say no if offered a drink or drugs at a party.
5. The author shared in this chapter why he chooses not to drink. Have you made that same decision? Why or why not?

Special Experience:
Visit a local Alateen meeting or Adolescent Treatment Center and ask to interview a couple of the kids who are trying to get unhooked and recover from drug and alcohol abuse.

Related Scripture:
Proverbs 20:1
Romans 13:13,14
1 Corinthians 6:19,20
1 Peter 4:7

Chapter 13
Sexual Abuse

The Big Idea:
Sexual abuse is one of society's deepest, darkest secrets and is much more prevalent than many think. If you or a friend of yours has experienced this trauma, then you must get help immediately.

Discussion Starters:
1. Were you surprised by the statistics quoted in this book?
2. Do you know anyone who has been sexually abused but has not talked to a parent, pastor or counselor? If so, please convince them to get help.
3. Read Psalm 23. How does this well-known Psalm give comfort to those who hurt?
4. What precautions can you take in your own life to keep from being sexually abused?
5. List the name(s) of at least one person you would immediately talk to if you ever had a problem with sexual abuse.

Special Experience:
Go to the public library and prepare a report about sexual abuse in order to learn the facts. Or call a local Child Sexual Abuse hot line (you'll find it in your phone book) and ask them to make a presentation at your church or school. They will also send you free literature about this important subject.

Related Scripture:
Isaiah 54:10
Matthew 28:20
Hebrews 13:5
James 1:5

Jim Burns is president of the National Institute of Youth Ministry. NIYM is an organization training adults who work closely with youth to help teens make positive decisions during the critical years of adolescence and prevent crisis situations in the home.

For more information about the National Institute of Youth Ministry, or for information regarding videos, books, educational programs or other resources for parents, teens or youth workers, write or call:

The National Institute of Youth Ministry
940 Calle Amanecer #G
San Clemente, CA 92673
(714) 498-4418

Resources Youth Can Grow On!

Stomping Out the Darkness
*Neil T. Anderson
& Dave Park*

Here is the powerful message from **Victory over the Darkness** written especially for young people. Provides youth with keys to their identity, worth, and acceptance as children of God.

Paperback
ISBN 08307.16408
Study Guide
ISBN 08307.17455

Getting Ready for the Guy/Girl Thing
*Greg Johnson
& Susie Shellenberger*

Wisdom to help 5th to 8th graders form godly relationships.

Paperback
ISBN 08307.14855

Radical Christianity
Jim Burns

Get down to core issues of how teens can make their lives count for Christ. You'll get hands-on, interactive chapters that cover topics like priorities, the cost of discipleship, integrity and more!

Paperback
ISBN 08307.17927
Video Seminar
SPCN 85116.01082

Radical Love
Jim Burns

The very best in life comes by following God's plan. Here's a frank discussion of things that today's youth are facing—like relationships and sex—and how to find God's best.

Paperback
ISBN 08307.17935
Video Seminar
SPCN 85116.00922

What Hollywood Won't Tell You About Sex, Love and Dating
*Greg Johnson
& Susie Shellenberger*

Youth learn things like how to have a conversation with someone of the opposite sex. It is possible.

Paperback
ISBN 08307.16777

So What's a Christian Anyway?

A fun and simple way to explain the basics of Christianity to youth. It's a 32-page comic-book size evangelism tool.

Paperback
ISBN 08307.13972

90 Days Through the New Testament
Jim Burns

A 90-day growth experience through the New Testament that lays the foundation for developing a daily time with God.

Paperback
ISBN 08307.14561

What the Bible is All About for Young Explorers
Frances Blankenbaker

The basics of *What the Bible Is All About*, in a format designed to make the Bible more approachable for youth.

Hardcover • ISBN
08307.11791

Ask for these resources at your local Christian bookstore.

Gospel Light

Give Youth the Word

YouthBuilders Group Bible Studies

These high-involvement, discussion-oriented, Bible-centered studies work together to give you a comprehensive program, seeing your young people through their high school years—and beyond. From respected youth worker Jim Burns.

The Word on:

The Word on: Sex, Drugs & Rock 'N' Roll
ISBN 08307.16424

Prayer and the Devotional Life
ISBN 08307.16432

Basics of Christianity
ISBN 08307.16440

Being a Leader, Serving Others & Sharing Your Faith
ISBN 08307.16459

Helping Friends in Crisis
ISBN 08307.16467

The Life of Jesus
ISBN 08307.16475

Finding and Using Your Spiritual Gifts
ISBN 08307.17897

The Sermon on the Mount
ISBN 08307.17234

Spiritual Warfare
ISBN 08307.17242

The New Testament
ISBN 08307.17250

The Old Testament
ISBN 08307.17269

Junior High Builders

Each reproducible manual has 13 Bible studies with games, activities and clip art for handouts.

Christian Basics
ISBN 08307.16963

The Life and Times of Jesus Christ
ISBN 08307.16971

The Parables of Jesus
ISBN 08307.16998

Growing as a Christian
ISBN 08307.17005

Christian Relationships
ISBN 08307.17013

Symbols of Christ
ISBN 08307.17021

The Power of God
ISBN 08307.17048

Faith in Action
ISBN 08307.17056

Peace, Love and Truth
ISBN 08307.17064

Great Old Testament Leaders
ISBN 08307.17072

Great Truths from Ephesians
ISBN 08307.17080

Lifestyles of the Not-So-Famous from the Bible
ISBN 08307.17099

Ask for these resources at your local Christian bookstore.

Gospel Light